"June Hunt says, 'There ar  iose who have grown hopeless.' This that once seemed forever lost. With a counseling to her credit, June shov promises of God."

**Sam Johnson**, U.S. Congressman, former Vietnam Prisoner of War

"If your world seems to be spinning out of control into nightmarish chaos, June Hunt shows you where to find stability and safety in her excellent book. Filled with Scripture, *Hope for Your Heart* gently guides readers to important anchors from God's Word which inspire, refresh, and instruct. Thank you, June!"

**Joni Eareckson Tada**, Founder & CEO, Joni & Friends International Disability Center

"As a pastor I have noticed two responses to difficult times—survival or revival. Survivors hunker down and wish things were different. Revivers trust God and take action, spreading hope to others as they pursue the promises of God. June Hunt has always been a reviver, offering hope to thousands through her writings and radio ministry. In *Hope for Your Heart*, June reveals how anyone can be a reviver. Read this book and let the revival begin."

**Gary Brandenburg**, Senior Pastor, Fellowship Bible Church, Dallas

"June's powerful teaching transcends cultural barriers, revealing the invincible power of God to transform lives. No matter who or *where* you are—and no matter where you've been—*Hope for Your Heart* shows how to anchor your life with biblical hope."

**Enkelejda Kumaraku**, Founder, Director & Host, *Radio 7* & *Media 7* television, Albania

"Hope is more than wishful thinking . . . more than deep desire. It's a reality that we can stake our lives on. June shows—step by step—how to have what the Bible calls the *hope that does not disappoint us.*"

**Kay Coles James,** Founder & President, The Gloucester Institute; Former Director of the U.S. Office of Personnel Management

"It's been said a person can live "bout forty days without food, seven days without water, eight minutes without air, but not a moment without hope.' If you struggle with feeling hopeless, don't wait another moment to find *Hope for your Heart.* It's here . . . on every page!"

**Zig Ziglar,** author/motivational teacher; Chairman, Zig Ziglar Corporation

# HOPE FOR YOUR HEART

## Also by June Hunt

*Bonding with Your Teen through Boundaries*
*Caring for a Loved One with Cancer*
*Counseling Through Your Bible Handbook*
*How to Forgive . . . When You Don't Feel Like It*
*How to Handle Your Emotions*
*How to Rise Above Abuse*
*Keeping Your Cool . . . When Your Anger Is Hot!*
*Seeing Yourself Through God's Eyes*

# HOPE

*for Your*

# HEART

*Finding Strength in Life's Storms*

## June Hunt

**:: CROSSWAY**

WHEATON, ILLINOIS

ISBN-13: 978-1-4335-0397-9
ISBN-10: 1-4335-0398-0
PDF ISBN: 978-1-4335-2687-9
Mobipocket ISBN: 978-1-4335-2688-6
ePub ISBN: 978-1-4335-2689-3

**Library of Congress Cataloging-in-Publication Data**
Hunt, June
    Hope for your heart : finding strength in life's storms / June Hunt.
      p. cm.
    Includes bibliographical references.
    ISBN 10: 1-4335-0398-0 ISBN 13: 978-1-4335-0397-9
    ISBN 13: 978-1-4335-2687-9 ISBN 13: 978-1-4335-2688-6
    1. Consolation. 2. Hope—Religious aspects—Christianity.
I. Title II. Title.
BV4909.H753      2011
248.8'6—dc22                  2010032012

Crossway is a publishing ministry of Good News Publishers.

| DP | | 20 | 19 | 18 | 17 | 16 | 15 | 14 | 13 | 12 | 11 |
|----|----|----|----|----|----|----|----|----|----|----|----|
| 15 | 14 | 13 | 12 | 11 | 10 | 9 | 8 | 7 | 6 | 5 | 4 | 3 | 2 | 1 |

## To

## Hannah Till

"*Promise me you will pray for my children*," my mother pleaded after doctors exhausted all treatment options and released her to hospice care. "I will," her best friend Hannah promised.

And within months my precious mother entered heaven.

Today if I were asked, "What is the greatest gift someone could give you?" my answer would be, "Genuinely pray for me!" Meanwhile, not a day goes by that Hannah Till doesn't lift me up to the throne of Grace, asking God to give me "help in time of need" (Heb. 4:16 ESV). Just knowing this gives me hope for my heart!

Hannah knows what it means to hold on to hope . . . to persevere through storms . . . to live an anchored life. Her knowledge of hope comes not from hearsay but from a lifetime of grabbing hold of and hanging on to the promises of God amidst pounding hailstorms that would have shipwrecked the hopes of many.

Hannah's inspirational husband, Lee Roy, was the gifted minister of music at one of America's largest churches, overseeing twenty-one choirs and a seventy-five-piece orchestra. But one February evening in 1972, the lives of the Till family changed forever—forty-four-year-old Lee Roy suffered a severe stroke.

Hannah and her three children rushed to his side as he lapsed in and out of a coma. While Lee Roy ultimately regained some of his speech and motor abilities, he was never able to work again. All these years Hannah has tenderly served Lee Roy while she herself weathered three cancer surgeries and partial loss of eyesight.

"My mother was strong, young, and vibrant—the head of the children's choir at church," says daughter and concert soloist Jenni. "Because she's known great loss, God uses her to give great hope to those with broken hearts. Her own challenges bring credibility to everything about which she testifies."

Daughter Hannah Beth explains, "Mother's ministry is serving as a surrogate mother to so many. She prays for people in need, following through to check on them, helping any way she can. She's an eternal matriarch!"

"Mother is truly the most giving person I've ever known," adds son Robert. "Because of Dad's illness, my parents had little. So they prayed and watched God provide. And when He did, mother often gave much away to those whose needs were greater than hers."

Hannah once told me, "I've never asked why. I just ask, 'What do You want from me today, Lord?' When I see Him in heaven, I'm not going to ask why. I'm going to kneel at His feet and sing praises to Him. I don't need to know why."

For the last fifty years, I have known hope—and her name is Hannah.

# CONTENTS

Acknowledgments     11

### PART ONE
*The Reasons for Hope — Guaranteed*

Introduction: Hope Starts Here     15

1   The Ultimate Life Preserver     19
    Hope Dispels Your Darkness
    *Hope: Tracking the Storms*

2   When Trouble Hits Wave upon Wave     31
    Hope Transforms Your Thinking
    *Transformed: A Boat without a Rudder/A Ship without a Sail*

3   Your Unfailing Anchor     45
    Hope Holds You Firmly Secure
    *Security: Outmaneuvering the Enemy*

4   The Flash Floods of Affliction     61
    Hope Teaches You to Trust
    *Trust: Caught in the Rip Current*

5   The Tidal Waves of Trouble     77
    Hope Arms You for Adversity
    *Trials: Anchored in Iceberg Alley*

### PART TWO
*The Sources of Hope — Guaranteed*

6   Trust in the Captain's Course     91
    Hope in the Sovereignty of God
    *The Sovereignty of God: Keeping an Even Keel*

7   An Anchor like No Other     103
    Hope in the Savior, Jesus
    *Jesus: A Star to Steer By*

8   The Right Map Will Light Your Way     121
    Hope in the Word of God
    *God's Word: A Map to Navigate By*

9   Knowing How to Navigate     137
    Hope in the Power of Prayer
    *Prayer: The Disastrous Dive—Redeemed*

PART THREE
*The Benefits of Hope — Guaranteed*

10  A Wreck Reclaimed                                         151
    Hope in the Gift of Grace
    *Grace: Finding Hidden Treasure*

11  Charting Your Course                                      163
    Hope to Pinpoint Your Purpose
    *Purpose: Taking a Different Tack*

12  Untangling Your Knots                                     175
    Hope to Be Free . . . by Forgiving
    *Forgiveness: Batten Down the Hatches*

13  Your Next Port: Paradise                                  187
    Hope to Inherit Heaven
    *Heaven: When the Seas Will Cease*

14  When Sea Billows Roll                                     197
    Hope to Possess Perfect Peace
    *Where Is Your Hope?*

Epilogue: How to Know Your Anchor Will Hold                   207

Notes                                                        209

About the Author                                             217

# ACKNOWLEDGMENTS

This book would not have set sail without all hands on deck—and what capable, creative hands! Thank you to those who provided valuable contributions on all things nautical—from the anatomy of boats to the physics of anchors!

Brent Ray first launched the idea of providing a book on hope to help a sea of people live an anchored life.

Elizabeth Cunningham, Jill Prohaska, Barbara Spruill, and Keith Wall skillfully buoyed the manuscript with countless ideas, rewrites, and edits.

Angie White ran a tight ship to deliver the right cargo to the right port.

Bea Garner, Jeanne Sloan, Beth Stapleton, Connie Steindorf, Carolyn White, Karen Williams, Laura Lyn Benoit, and Phillip Bleecker—awash in an ocean of manuscript versions—continued proofing, reviewing, keying, and checking from stem to stern until journey's end.

Josh Dennis and Ben Parail floated one cover image after another until we sailed into the sunset.

Titus O'Bryant battened down the hatches on citations and research.

Kay Deakins faithfully cleared the decks for me so this project could stay afloat.

Al Fisher at Crossway trusted me to weather the storms of writing in spite of several setbacks, and Ted Griffin kept the wind in the sails of the manuscript after it left our hands.

And I must add that Jesus has been my strong, personal Anchor. Because of His life in me, I have an anchored life. He is why I have unbreakable, unshakable hope for my heart.

PART ONE

*The Reasons for Hope — Guaranteed*

# INTRODUCTION:
# HOPE STARTS HERE

Confession is good for the soul, and I have a whopper: I named our biblical counseling ministry HOPE FOR THE HEART . . . I often tell callers on our call-in radio broadcast, HOPE IN THE NIGHT, to "hang on to *hope*" . . . I have taught Bible studies on the topic of *hope* . . . and I have an office chock-full of mementos bearing the word *hope*. Yet, for years if you had asked me point-blank, "June, what *is* hope?" I couldn't have told you!

Oh, I had a definition of hope, but that's not the same as having a handle on hope.

Back then, hope was an elusive concept to me . . . cloud-like . . . impossible to grab hold of. Sure, I was familiar with Scriptures like Romans 5:5 that say, "Hope does not disappoint us." But still the word *hope*, in and of itself, is always inspiring! It is encouraging, heartening, and reassuring. Hope is something we all want . . . and something we all *need*. But. . . .

Hope is what every mountain climber possesses at the bottom of the mountain. Imagine looking up at the tallest peak, believing, *With enough determination I can make it to the top*!

Imagine starting out at the bottom of the mountain *full of hope*. You begin to ascend step by step and traverse from side to side . . . and soon you find yourself on a severe slope, still *holding on to hope*. As you plant your foot, the rock gives way and your foot slips . . . you start to slide, reach out, grab hold of a bush . . . and now you're *hanging on to hope*!

After once again getting your footing, each step brings you closer to the top until finally you see the summit. You ascend to the top and experience *hope fulfilled*!

That's the outcome for which every mountain climber *hopes*. But the truth is, this kind of hope is not enough; it's not assured.

A successful climb is *not guaranteed*, regardless of how much hope a climber may have. Accidents happen. Equipment fails. People die. *Even though we all want to be hopeful, what can we actually count on? I wondered. What can we stake our lives on?*

I lived with these baffling questions for decades . . . until 2006, when God graciously began to connect the dots. It started as I prepared to teach a *Hope Biblical Counseling Institute* for nine hours on the topic of . . . you guessed it . . . hope!

During the *Institute*, I expected to explain "definitions, characteristics, causes, and steps to solutions" before an audience of pastors, counselors, teachers, and other interested individuals. There was just one problem. How could I ever *hope* to teach something I didn't fully understand myself?

So I called my pastor . . . a brilliant, scholarly man who had at one time headed a major denomination. "June," he confided, "you have your hands full this time. In my opinion hope is the hardest topic to preach on. It's elusive . . . difficult to describe . . . hard to handle."

Next I checked with a professor at one of the country's leading seminaries. "It's one of the hardest topics anyone can ever speak on," he told me. "When you try to separate hope from the topic you need hope for . . . like hope for marriage or hope for finances or hope for overcoming addictions . . . you're left with a major challenge. It's like trying to catch the wind."

Undaunted, I continued to interview, read, and research, surveying every single verse in Scripture having anything to do with the word or concept of hope. During this process I reread Hebrews 6:19: "We have this hope as an anchor for the soul, firm and secure." And that's when it hit me. . . .

## ANCHOR

Hope is an anchor! And anchors are tangible. I figured that if I understood anchors, they would help me understand hope.

That hopeful realization launched me on a voyage to learn everything I could about anchors. I researched anchors . . . asked seafaring friends about anchors . . . read books about anchors . . . studied diagrams of anchors. Sure enough, what had once been as murky as the depths of a churning ocean slowly began to grow clear.

*Everyone needs an anchor.*

A famous and rather amusing quote by Benjamin Franklin reads, "In this life nothing is certain but death and taxes."

I'd like to add one more certainty to the list: storms.

I'm not thinking about literal storms with thunder and lightning and gale-force winds, although they are just as certain as death and taxes. I am referring to those heavy, dark clouds that roll into our lives and unleash torrents of trouble and trauma.

These storms can be like squalls, suddenly and powerfully blowing in setbacks and sorrow. They contain downpours that can saturate our days with disappointment and devastating heartache.

Failure . . . betrayal . . . abuse . . . disaster . . . death . . . the list of potential storms could go on and on, and there's not one of us who at some time or another hasn't felt swept away by them.

Through my research, reading, and prayer, God graciously granted me a life-changing discovery: The hope that is discussed so extensively in the Bible has nothing to do with crossing our fingers and hoping for the best. *Authentic biblical hope is a powerful, undergirding force—an anchor able to sustain us through the fiercest storms.*

Men and women down through the centuries have clung to biblical hope when barraged by the biting winds and tumultuous tides of life's storms. And the world simply watched in amazement when knees didn't buckle and faith didn't quaver.

That's because *biblical hope is based on the promises of God.* In fact, the biblical writers applied hope to a considerable number of situations and circumstances and watched God move in miraculous ways.

So what about you? What's your situation as you open this book? Maybe you are in the midst of a violently swirling storm that you feel is about to take you under. Perhaps you're trying to help someone else weather a storm. Or could it be that you've been through some storms with hurricane-force winds and want to be prepared for the ones brewing just over the horizon?

Whatever the case, this book is all about the one resource that will hold you steady and keep you standing when the storms of life engulf you emotionally, physically, and spiritually. It is not only a resource, it is a gift . . . given by God's outstretched hand to you. And that gift is *hope.*

In the chapters ahead we'll explore the depths of this essential virtue and closely examine its vital role in holding us fast when life's storms rumble and rage. Along the way I believe you'll come to see that when you have authentic biblical hope you will have something no person or situation can ever take away—you will have *an anchored life.*

We have this hope as an anchor for the soul, firm and secure. (Heb. 6:19)

# 1

# THE ULTIMATE
# LIFE PRESERVER

## HOPE DISPELS YOUR DARKNESS

---

*Hope:*
*Tracking the Storms*

---

Years ago I received a phone call asking for help. "June, I have a niece in her thirties who moved here from Florida. She works at a hospital . . . she's single and really needs friends. Do you have any ideas?"

"Well, I teach a Bible study for singles," I answered, "and we're like a family. In fact, we don't even take spring or summer breaks or stop for holidays; that's how much we value and support one another. I teach a group on Sunday mornings at my church, and then on Tuesday evenings we meet at my home. About sixty to eighty come from all over the area. We'd love to have her join us."

Her aunt was elated, and the following evening Sandra walked through the door of my home and into my life.

She became a consistent part of our regular group, enjoying the inductive Bible study, and she was growing spiritually. As she absorbed more biblical truth, I began to see a change in her.

## A FLOOD TIDE OF PAIN

Tuesday evenings fell into a pattern: The end of our music/message time ushered in the warm glow of our food/fellowship time. It was understood that anyone could stay longer for deeper conversation, which sometimes stretched into the wee hours. One evening Sandra waited until everyone else had trickled out. As we sat on the couch, her expression turned to one of distress. "June, I don't know what to do. I've been having these horrible flashbacks."

"What kind of flashbacks?" I probed.

"Oh, they're . . . bad," she whispered.

"Are they sexual?"

Taking a deep breath, she whispered, "Yes."

Seeing she was on the verge of tears, I reached out and gently took her hand. Several moments passed in silence as she struggled to collect her thoughts.

Sandra swallowed hard. Then slowly, haltingly she began pouring out her pain. For more than a month she had been flooded with disturbing, disgusting images of being sexually abused by her father. Many different scenes played in her mind like a vile movie . . . so real, so lurid, so sordid. She hadn't wanted to tell anyone, but her secret had become too much to bear.

"June, I think I'm . . . losing my mind," she shuddered, tears spilling from her eyes.

The sexual victimization in her early childhood had caused a repression of painful memories. This phenomenon, called dissociation, is not uncommon as the mind puts up a protective barrier to shield the child victim from the excruciating pain of traumatic experiences. Typically many years, even decades, pass before the buried memories begin to surface. Often people in their late twenties and thirties begin to have flashbacks of past trauma.

"I feel like I'm walking right on the edge," she told me. "One slip and I'm going over."

"Sandra, you can get back on solid ground," I assured her.

Sandra had up to that point functioned quite well. She worked successfully as a medical professional and had a moderate social life. But now the more her memories stirred, the more her emotions erupted. Sandra's heart was flooded with feelings of anger, betrayal, and anguish. Ultimately she felt *helpless*, knowing she couldn't erase the past, and she felt *hopeless*, believing she had no future.

## HOPE HELD AT ARM'S LENGTH

Sandra was starting to drown in hopelessness. What she needed was the ultimate life preserver . . . *hope* . . . to assure her that God's help and healing were within her reach.

"I can't handle these flashbacks," she said with a resigned sense of defeat.

"Yes, you can," I countered. "You *can* get through this difficult time. I want you to claim the Bible promise, 'I can do all things through Christ who strengthens me.'"[1]

"It won't work for me," she insisted.

"Do you believe the Bible is true?" I asked, knowing her answer would be yes.

"Do you believe the Bible is the Word of God?"

"Yes."

"Do you believe God would lie to you?"

"No."

Then I explained, "Whenever you feel like giving up, I want you to claim Philippians 4:13 (NKJV), 'I can do all things through Christ who strengthens me.' Christ will empower you to do it. Christ, who lives in you, will be the power source for you. It won't be easy, but you have the power of God within you. He is your Redeemer, and He can redeem your past—as painful as it is and as impossible as that may seem right now."

She looked away. "That will work for you, June, but not for me. I'm just not good enough."

"Oh, Sandra, it's not about being good enough or strong enough or anything else enough!" I responded. "It's about receiving God's compassion, hope, and healing. His *hope* for your heart is based on His *promises* for your life. His *hope* for your future is based on His *plan* for your future. The Lord Himself says in Jeremiah 29:11, 'I know the plans I have for you . . . plans to prosper you and not to harm you, plans to give you hope and a future.'"

## THE DOWNWARD SPIRAL

I was painfully aware that my pleas, along with God's promises, had fallen on deaf ears. It was as though Sandra had shut off emotionally, and she was spiraling downward. She saw no future. Instead she was a prisoner of her past.

I met frequently with Sandra over the next few months, but she seemed to be sinking down into the darkest sea. All of my attempts to pull her up and out were in vain, and outside counseling wasn't proving to be helpful.

She cut herself off from nearly all of her friends and stopped attending our Bible study. Gradually she started drowning. She began drinking heavily, no doubt to numb her emotional pain. Disappearing for long stretches, she finally reemerged . . . but engulfed in a continual flow of sadness. Sandra was totally submerged in her painful past, the ultimate life preserver—hope—seemingly a thousand miles from her grasp.

Then one day I received a telephone call from the hospital where she worked. Sandra was in the hospital . . . *as a patient*. She had attempted suicide.

When I first arrived at the hospital, she said, "It's bizarre to be in the place where I've come to work a thousand times . . . and now here I am in the psych ward!"

We talked candidly about her attempt . . . about her pain . . . about her past. And as I left, I thought, *Fortunately she's in a safe place . . . they'll get her back on track*. I felt confident she would move toward wholeness.

But after several months Sandra's story took an unexpected turn. Her insurance ran out. She would be moved to the state hospital, thirty miles outside Dallas.

The very next day after her transfer, my telephone rang. "June, you have to get me out of here!"

"What's happened? Is something the matter?" I never will forget her exact words.

"June, I'm not like these people. They are walking zombies. I am not a zombie! I don't belong here! You have to get me out of here!"

"Sandra, I . . . I . . . I don't have the authority to do that," I stammered.

"Oh yes you do! Just come and get me."

"I don't think I can. I wouldn't even know what to do."

"June, drive here, come to the front, and we'll walk out together. They can't hold me against my will!"

Later Sandra called again, "June . . . you have to get me out of here. You have to come and get me!"

"Sandra, I don't know that it's right for me to do that."

"June," she said next, "I've been thinking about what you've said." I could hardly believe what rolled off her tongue then.

"I remember when you quoted the verse, 'I can do all things through Christ who strengthens me.'" (What a surprise to hear her quote Scripture!) "Well, I know that's true. And I do realize that the Lord really does have plans for me. He has hope and a future for me." (I was astounded to hear her saying the actual words from Jeremiah 29:11.)

"And I've been thinking, God promises to give me peace that passes all understanding." (She was quoting Philippians 4:7. I could hardly believe my ears!)

"June, I've been thinking about what God says . . . that God loves me and that He'll never leave me or forsake me. . . . I am a child of God."

She was quoting Deuteronomy and the Gospel of John! She was repeating back everything I'd been saying. All along I thought my words weren't even going in her ears, much less penetrating her heart.

"You know, I've been thinking, I need to trust in the Lord with all my heart. I shouldn't rely on my own understanding. He promises to direct my path." (Amazing! That was Proverbs 3:5–6. Yes, that was exactly what she needed to do!)

To be absolutely candid, I didn't think the answer to Sandra's problems would be found in a mental institution or through more drugs. I learned she was not getting the kind of in-depth counseling she needed to process her pain and give her hope for her distraught heart.

After much prayer, I made my decision. It was Friday afternoon, and our group was having a two-day Bible study/fun/fellowship retreat. So I drove to the state hospital and picked up Sandra as she had asked. We went to the retreat, and I had absolute peace that this was right.

The retreat was a rich time of spiritual feeding and fellowship for Sandra and for our entire group. Then on Monday morning we both met with a renowned Christian psychiatrist, who immediately took her off several medications, believing she was overmedicated. In addition to setting her up with a Christian counselor to help process her pain, a friend from our Bible study, a caring doctor's wife, came alongside to consistently encourage Sandra.

Consequently she felt less and less hopeless . . . and more and more hopeful in her heart. The ultimate life preserver securely encircled Sandra, holding her up in this darkest and roughest of seas.

## HOW TO MAKE HOPE "WORK"

Think seriously about this question: When someone is in the depths of depression and is struggling with the will to live, what does that struggler need most? What is the single most important "ingredient" for you to give? If you had to give an answer, what would you say?

Genuine concern? Empathy? Compassion?

Total acceptance? Unconditional love?

My personal thought would be *truth*. And the reason should be obvious. Jesus says, "The truth will set you free."[2]

I had been speaking the truth *to* Sandra . . . she even had the truth *in* her . . . but she was not free. This mystified me. What was the problem? What did she not have?

*Hope!* She didn't have *hope* . . . she didn't have *hope for her heart*. You can have all the truth in your head, but it must also be in your heart through hope.

Sandra knew a lot of *truth*, but didn't have *hope* that the truth would work for her. Truth alone does not set you free. Many people have acquired *information*, but they need *transformation*. Why?

Sandra needed to not only *know* the truth of God's promise for her . . . she also needed to have *hope* that those promises were for her. And that hope saved her life!

## IT'S ALL IN A NAME

One fall day in 1985 my friend Jan and I decided to start a new Christian radio ministry . . . and we needed the perfect name. We knew we would be discussing relevant topics with real solutions.

I remember thinking about the word *Kaleidoscope* (for the variety of topics we would cover) and *Point-Counterpoint* (because of our two viewpoints).

Suddenly Sandra came to mind . . . Sandra whose life was almost snuffed out simply because she had no hope. Then I thought about the thousands of Sandras . . . men, women, teens, and children . . . who need hope! We decided to name the ministry after what we knew everyone needed: HOPE FOR THE HEART.

The signature Scripture for our ministry is taken from the promise spoken by the Lord Himself: "I know the plans I have for you . . . plans to prosper you and not to harm you, plans to give you hope and a future" (Jer. 29:11).

Do you realize what those words spoken by the Lord mean for your life? You have been given a guaranteed hope because it is not based on you. You have a guaranteed hope that is:

- planned by God,
- prosperous for your life,
- promised for your future.

This is His plan for you, not your plans, and thus it is guaranteed by God. What comfort!

This is His hope for you, not your hope, and thus it is guaranteed by God. What relief!

This is His future for you, not your future, and thus it is guaranteed by God. What joy!

## EVERYONE NEEDS AN ANCHOR

No sailor survives at sea without an anchored ship—the ultimate life preserver—and no traveler on the sea of life survives without an anchored life.

What an anchor is to a ship, hope is to the soul. Both ships and souls are kept safe by a firm, secure anchor that keeps holding despite turbulent winds and churning tides.

The Bible says this about Jesus: "We have this hope as an anchor for the soul, firm and secure" (Heb. 6:19). This means that every authentic Christian has been given such an anchor in Christ.

We've all been in the same boat with cloudy thinking about hope. What we need is clear thinking about what hope is and what it isn't. I believe there are two kinds of hope: cultural hope and Christian hope.

The common understanding of hope is quite different from the Christian meaning as taught in the Bible. If you live by the cultural meaning of hope, the kind of hope espoused by most people in our world, you may only have a boatful of unfounded optimism and wishful thinking. What you hope for will sometimes happen, and at other times it won't.

When we live with Christian or biblical hope, we have an anchored life. We are held steady in the midst of any storm. The Bible says that when your hope is anchored in God, He will teach you His truth and will lead you in the way you should go. This prayer is yours to claim: "Guide me in your truth and teach me, for you are God my Savior, and my hope is in you all day long" (Ps. 25:5).

## HOW TO GET A HANDLE ON HOPE

*Cultural hope* is an optimistic desire that something will be fulfilled. This kind of hope is unsteady and uncertain because it is based on changeable people and circumstances. People often say things like, "I hope I get the job" or "I hope she gets a scholarship" or "I hope he wins the next election." These desires, to a large degree, are beyond our control.

Even the things we like to think we have control over (health, finances, home) can be greatly affected by factors outside our grasp. Even the forces of nature can intervene and dash our hopes. Cultural hope can lead to devastating disappointment. And if our spiritual priorities are off, the Bible says, "Such is the destiny of all who forget God; so perishes the hope of the godless" (Job 8:13).

*Christian hope* is a guaranteed assurance that something will be fulfilled. This hope is not subject to change because it is anchored in our unchangeable God. That's why the writer of Hebrews said, "Faith is being *sure* of what we *hope* for and certain of what we do not see" (Heb. 11:1). When Paul said that Christians have the "hope of eternal life" (Titus 1:2; 3:7), he meant we have the *guaranteed assurance, the full confidence, the certainty* of eternal life.

The believer's hope is based on the Bible, God's unchanging Word. When you feel uncertain about life . . . adrift on an unclear course . . . the Lord wants you to rely on *His promises* and to have endurance based on *His provision.* He will not fail you, even when you don't understand the "whys" of what's happening in your life. The psalmist was mindful of God's promise: "Sustain me according to your promise, and I will live; do not let my *hopes* be dashed" (Ps. 119:116).

This hope provides all the certainty you will ever need. As the apostle Paul said, "Everything that was written in the past was written to teach us, so that through endurance and the encouragement of the Scriptures we might have *hope*" (Rom. 15:4). In short, Christian hope is:

- *not* dependent on another person or a group of people, but rather is dependent on the Lord alone.
- *not* wishful thinking, vague longing, or trying to fulfill a dream, but rather is assured, unchangeable, and absolute.
- *not* determined by circumstances, events, or abilities, but rather is based on what is secured and promised.
- *not* merely a desire, but rather the delayed fulfillment of reality.
- *not* relying on the stars, luck, chance, or timing, but rather is predestined and settled in the heart and mind of God.
- *not* hoping your good will outweigh your bad to get you to heaven, but rather is the certainty of God that you will go to heaven.

In him we were also chosen, having been predestined according to the plan of him who works out everything in conformity with the purpose of his will. (Eph. 1:11)

## POWERFUL PROMISES

The noun *hope* in the New Testament is the Greek word *elpis*, which means "favorable and confident expectation" and always relates to "the unseen and to the future."[3] Although certain translations of the Bible use the word *hope* from both the cultural and Christian perspectives, the undeniable focus of spiritual hope is *guaranteed hope in God and in His promises.*

But can we always be sure that Christian hope is *guaranteed*, 100 percent of the time? Christian hope can sound beyond belief . . . unreal . . . far-fetched. Nevertheless, you can have absolute confidence in the promises of God simply because they *are* the promises of God, and He has proven Himself time and time again. They are not the promises of a finite, frail human being, but they are the promises of an infinite, all-powerful God.

It is impossible for any human being to resurrect someone from the dead or part the sea in half or calm a raging storm or save a soul from hell. But it is no challenge for the Creator of life to save life or to restore life. Nothing is impossible to Him who holds all of creation in the palm of His hand. He knows the subconscious thoughts and the secret intentions of every heart.

He who spoke the world into existence can certainly keep His word to those whom He created, loves, and sustains. Furthermore, He is Truth and cannot tell a lie. His words and His promises are sure. The Bible gives this assurance: "It is impossible for God to lie" (Heb. 6:18).

He is the ultimate life preserver. My hope and prayer today is that the Sandras of this world will find true hope in Christ, their unfailing Anchor.

Our true Anchor, Christ, guarantees us hope in any situation because He is in control . . . not circumstances, not people. We can have an unfailing hope because Jesus is our unfailing Anchor.

# Anchoring Your Hope: Tracking the Storm

Hearing "A storm is coming!" on a newscast can be helpful in planning your day. Especially if you don't want your hopes to be dashed by a downpour when you're taking a hike or a trip to the park. Maybe the next day will be better. But how much do you know about storms? How do you know if a storm is serious?

For most people, storms are merely dark clouds, thunderclaps, and a short rain shower. Few people know about other kinds of storms, such as cyclones, typhoons, and hurricanes.

Just for clarification, let's understand certain terms:

- *Cyclones* are storms with a closed system of winds that rotate clockwise south of the equator and counterclockwise in the Northern Hemisphere.
- *Hurricanes/typhoons* are types of tropical cyclones in the Northern Hemisphere that have sustained winds of 74 mph or more. The term *hurricane* is used for cyclones east of the International Dateline, whereas *typhoon* refers to storms west of the International Dateline.

Most weather buffs know about the Saffir-Simpson Hurricane Scale developed in the early 1970s that details the wind speeds and storm surges associated within five categories. *Storm surge* refers to the abnormal rise in sea level caused by the force of a hurricane's spiraling wind. Vertically, a storm can surge over twenty feet and horizontally over several hundred miles. This scale is used to estimate the potential property damage and flooding expected along the coast when a hurricane hits land.

- Category 1—*Minimal*: 74–95 mph winds/4–5 foot storm surge
- Category 2—*Moderate*: 96–110 mph winds/6–8 foot storm surge
- Category 3—*Extensive*: 111–130 mph winds/9–12 foot storm surge
- Category 4—*Extreme*: 131–155 mph winds/13–18 foot storm surge
- Category 5—*Catastrophic*: 155+ mph winds/18+ foot storm surge

In 1989, Category 4 Hurricane Hugo battered Charlotte, North Carolina—a city 175 miles *inland*. Its 100 mph winds destroyed buildings, downed power lines, and uprooted trees, turning small items left outside into flying missiles.[4]

Compared to those figures, tropical depressions (0–38 mph winds) and tropical storms (39–73 mph winds/0–3 foot storm surge) seem mild. That's why when meteorologists give "storm warnings," the sense of urgency and precaution escalates along with the categories. You could probably withstand a tropical depression with little care, but when a Category 5 hurricane blows in, you'd better board up the windows, batten down the hatches, and hightail it out of there!

What is the difference between a hurricane watch and a hurricane warning? A *watch* reports that a storm will hit within thirty-six hours and a *warning* within twenty-four hours. Proverbs 22:3 says, "A prudent man sees danger and takes refuge, but the simple keep going and suffer for it."

Real-life storms are a lot like the meteorological kind. They come in various shapes, sizes, and severities. Sometimes we experience inconvenient "downpours" (flat tires, forgotten appointments, canceled flights). Sometimes we encounter a "squall" (major fights, job firing, forced relocation). Sometimes we are forced to endure a full-fledged "hurricane" (demoralizing abuse, devastating illness, divorce, death of a loved one). Our problems run the gamut.

Weathering storms could be frightening if it weren't for this rock-solid fact: We have a steadying force . . . One who gives us *steadfast* hope. With Christ as our personal Anchor, we are promised an anchored life. The psalmist said, "God is our refuge and strength, an ever-present help in trouble. Therefore we will not fear, though the earth give way and the mountains fall into the heart of the sea, though its waters roar and foam and the mountains quake with their surging."[5]

What type of storm are you facing? Christ Himself will be your hope. He knows how to give you strength.

He will be your personal Anchor and will hold you steady through the storm.

# 2

# WHEN TROUBLE HITS
# WAVE UPON WAVE

## HOPE TRANSFORMS YOUR THINKING

---

*Transformed:*
*A Boat without a Rudder/A Ship without a Sail*

---

*Do it, June! Drive off the bridge! It would be so easy! Why not?* How clearly I remember those desperate words, coursing through my mind on a cloudless summer day. As a newly licensed teen driver, I tightened my grip around the steering wheel of my car and seriously contemplated whether this was the day to bring a quick and welcome end to a life of just fifteen years.

My foot was poised on the accelerator, the compulsion to press down building, when all of a sudden I felt an overpowering restraint. *Wait! What if I'm not successful? I could end up only maiming myself. Then Mom would have the huge burden of needing to take care of me for the rest of my life!*

Looking back, I remember the painful emotions churning inside me and the hopelessness that wrought such upheaval in my life. It wasn't that I *wanted* to kill myself—I just wanted to stop the pain. Relentless, unspoken, soul-ravaging pain. Hopelessness had settled over my life like a dense, endless fog. Its source? My own, very personal, very private, four-letter word: h-o-m-e.

From the outside, my family *looked* like we had it all: a lovely house . . . a "successful" father . . . a gracious mother . . . four well-behaved children . . . a lifestyle of plenty. But locked inside the walls of that lovely house was an *unlovely* family dynamic, a secret life that ripped hope from my heart and dashed it to pieces like a sailboat in a tsunami.

## CRUELTY IN COLORADO

My story of chaos begins with my father. In his public life he was widely acclaimed as a successful businessman, but in our family he was chronically critical and cruel, hardly a "success."

We were a family "on the side"—my parents weren't married until I was age twelve. I'll never forget the time when I was eight years old, and my father, mother, brother, and I were on a rare vacation in Colorado Springs, Colorado. A couple my parents knew and their twelve-year-old daughter had joined us for the trip.

Rae Jean and I were in the far backseat of a big Suburban that my father had leased, while the adults occupied the seats in front of us. Cruising around town, Rae Jean began acting up, as restless and cooped-up young girls often do. Her squirrelly behavior went on for a while, until Dad finally reached his limit.

"Rae Jean," he shouted, "if you don't stop, I'm putting you out!"

Maybe she just thought it was an idle threat. Rae Jean didn't know that my dad's threats were never idle.

As for me, I was well aware of his temper, so I sat silently, motioning for her to settle down.

Sure enough, my dad braked to a stop on the side of the highway, stepped out of the car, and opened the rear door where Rae Jean sat.

"Out!" he yelled.

Once she was out of the car, my dad got back in and drove off. Her parents, undoubtedly fearful, sat silently as Rae Jean stood there, stunned, watching as the Suburban disappeared in the distance.

After driving around for a short while, my father circled back to retrieve Rae Jean from the side of the road where he had deposited her. Then, as Dad opened the door for Rae Jean to get in, he glared at me and said, "Now you, out!"

I was shocked and incensed even as a little child. Whatever he may have thought, I knew I was innocent. I wanted to say, "I didn't do anything wrong. I don't deserve to be put out!" But I had learned in my brief eight years that the only opinion that mattered was my father's, so I bit my tongue and climbed out of the car.

I assumed his plan of action would be the same for me as for Rae Jean. Well, I wasn't about to just stand there and wait for him to decide my fate. I looked around, picked my route, and started walking . . . away from the direction he had just taken.

Of course, being totally unfamiliar with my surroundings I had no destination in mind, but I was determined to show my dad that he wasn't in control . . . I was!

Night began to fall, and I found myself in a nice housing subdivision. I was naturally terrified but refused to show it, my anger and indignation still fueling my resolve. I decided to ask for help, so I picked a house that looked safe and knocked on the door. Fortunately, the kind couple living there took pity on me.

I couldn't remember the name of the hotel where we were staying. "Could you remember the hotel if we drove you around?" they asked. I didn't know, but when we walked into one certain lobby, I recognized the red carpet. There were my parents, waiting for me, with Dad acting as unsympathetic and unconcerned as ever.

Forcing me out of the car was, to me, a case of callous injustice and indifference. It was unfair and said to me, "You don't count. You're not really here." Dad was not interested in me or my feelings . . . or justice. This was a pervasive pattern in my home life.

The issue for me was feeling trapped . . . desperately wanting to get out, wanting something different, but being unable to escape. When Dad was demeaning, I didn't feel I could do anything. Everything seemed so fatalistic . . . so dark . . . so hopeless.

## DOMESTIC DYSFUNCTION

In addition to his harsh temperament, my father's unabashed lifestyle of infidelity took a terrible toll on our family . . . especially on my mother, who was half his age when they married. When they met, he already had a wife and six children, the second-born the same age as my mother.

I believe that by marrying my dad, Mother was attempting to fill a father void in her heart, created by her own father's death when she was three years old. Even after becoming aware that their relationship was wrong, she succumbed to the lure of a persistent, persuasive father figure. My father was a very powerful man; few people *ever* told him no.

Dad was also excessively possessive of Mother. Beautiful, submissive, charming, she was the classic trophy wife. He proudly showed her off at his frequent dinner parties, where she shined like a lighthouse against the dark backdrop of his stormy disposition.

We four children were forbidden to speak at mealtimes ("Children are to be seen, not heard.") unless there was a topic of conversation that would be of interest to everyone. Since nothing we said was ever interesting to Dad, we rarely spoke.

I remember him often telling me, "You are a bad influence on your mother." At other times he would complain, "All of you children are a bad influence on your mother!" So immediately after dinner each night, we were ordered upstairs to our rooms. Further contact with Mother was forbidden.

Mother's heart ached over his possessiveness and prohibitions. After dinner she would use any excuse to embark on her nightly mission of shuttle diplomacy . . . clandestinely dashing upstairs to make the rounds room-by-room . . . checking on us, hugging us, encouraging us before returning to my father's side. Nurturing our tender hearts was her true priority, although he tried to deny her that right.

In truth, my mother and I experienced a role reversal as I tried to be her protector. But no matter how hard I worked at it, I didn't have the power to keep her safe. Sometimes when Dad would discover her crying over his flagrant adulterous indiscretions, he would come into my bedroom and dogmatically allege, "Your mother is mentally ill today."

Though outraged and incredulous over the callousness of his words, I knew I should take them seriously nonetheless. Dad's eldest son from his first marriage had been institutionalized for years, diagnosed as paranoid schizophrenic.

And though I knew tears were not a sign of mental illness and that my half-brother's diagnosis was completely legitimate, I also knew this: Dad had money; money buys power; power buys people. I was deathly afraid that Dad would pay a psychiatrist to institutionalize Mother.

Dad terrorized Mother not only by asserting that she was mentally ill but also by taking her to different psychiatrists. Although no doctor ever diagnosed her with any kind of mental disorder, just the mention of mental illness struck terror in her heart . . . and in mine.

## BANISHMENT

I lived in daily dread of what might happen to Mom. In the midst of one of his rampages about Mother's mental state, I lost it. "Has it ever occurred to you that *you* might be the one mentally ill?" I asked, seething with hatred.

Instantly my father retaliated physically. I was stunned. His actions struck me like a flash flood. Nevertheless, I was determined he would not make me cry, and he didn't. *I won* . . . until the next morning when my father sent me to boarding school for several months. I was only ten minutes away from home, but I might as well have been in Siberia.

For several summers I was also sent away to camp. To get to go to camp is one matter . . . being sent away to camp is another. Since this camp was in Colorado, every mention of Colorado evoked a sickening feeling. While at camp, I never knew if Mother would be permanently gone . . . institutionalized . . . when I returned home. For years I hated Colorado.

Only when Mom took us kids to her mother's in Idabel, Oklahoma, did I afford myself the luxury of relaxation and genuine carefree play with neighboring cousins. There I allowed myself to live, and there my mother also lived, because there my father was not around! But unfortunately we always went back home.

## THE ULTIMATE SOLUTION

The "bad influence" accusations . . . the threats to have Mom institutionalized . . . the isolation of boarding school . . . the exiles to summer camp . . . Dad's perpetual pummeling all led to a deepening sense of hopelessness and despair within me. When I felt I could bear it no longer, I approached Mother with a practical solution.

"I've figured out a way to kill Dad," I announced matter-of-factly. "There won't be much repercussion on me because I'm a minor." I was dead serious, but I'm so grateful for my mother's response. She did not chide me or laugh at me or ridicule me. Instead she gently and sympathetically said, "No, honey. I appreciate what you're trying to do, but that really won't be necessary."

My offer to kill Dad was not motivated by a desire to commit cold-blooded murder. Instead, like my impulse to drive off the bridge, it was motivated by utter hopelessness. I had lost hope that I would ever experience a home where I felt protected . . . where life was predictable . . . where justice prevailed . . . where I could be at peace.

## THE COMMON CORD OF HOPELESSNESS

Hopelessness, the kind I understand intuitively because of my growing-up years, is what motivates countless people across the United States and Canada to call me each weeknight during the live two-hour call-in counseling radio broadcast I host. Over the years I've received thousands of poignant and pain-filled calls on *HOPE IN THE NIGHT* . . . desperate cries from people struggling with all kinds of heartaches.

One of the most memorable conversations I've ever had involved a man named Tyler, an alcoholic unable to overcome his addiction. Because of his alcohol dependence and the resulting problems, his wife of twenty years had left him, and he had been divorced for six years.

Feeling utterly hopeless, he was on the verge of committing suicide. In fact, when he called me, Tyler had a loaded gun in his hand. Our unforgettable conversation unfolded like this:

*June, I want to end my life.*

What's so painful that you want to take your life?

*My ex-wife said, "If you ever drink again, I'll divorce you." I went to a treatment center, and I was sober for eight years. But I drank again and she divorced me.*

You're saying that you feel hooked, and you know the costs. . . . It cost you your marriage and . . .

*Counseling hasn't helped. I also pray and go to church, but the temptation is still there. What do I do?*

The apostle Paul said, "For I do not do the good I want, but the evil I do not want is what I keep on doing" (Rom. 7:19 ESV). And then he said, "Who will rescue me from this body of death?" (Rom. 7:24). There was a sense of desperation. Only a relationship with Christ could bring about real change. Tyler, God knows the pain in your heart, but He also says, "I know the plans I have for you . . . plans to prosper you . . . not to harm you, plans to give you hope and a future" (Jer. 29:11).

*I've been with God all of my life, but I've been an alcoholic for thirty-seven years. I've got two wonderful children I love, and I love my ex-wife too. Now I have nobody. For twenty years I raised my kids, but I wasn't really there because of my alcoholism. When the divorce finally went through, it just blew me away and right now I don't care.*

Do you have a plan for committing suicide?

*Yeah, I've got a gun sitting right here.*

How long have you had this plan?

*I've been thinking about it for the last twelve months. I have lived forty-nine years, and all those years have been hell. I've loved God, I know the Bible, I've asked God to help me so many times . . . but every time I pray for help, nothing happens.*

Let me ask you: Do you believe that Jesus is God?

*Yes, I do.*

When He was in the garden of Gethsemane, He prayed, "Let this cup pass from me."[1] If Jesus, who is God, prayed to the Father and that prayer was not answered, there was a more perfect will. We may not understand God's will at the time, but there is always a bigger picture that we can't see. You said you have children—how old are they?

*A daughter who is twenty-two and a son who's nineteen. I love them both. But I've burned so many bridges that I don't have anyone to grab onto.*

God has a plan for you, Tyler. There is a reason I asked about your son and daughter. You told me you love them very much. At times we think, *There is no hope for me. I don't have any choice.* When your kids and your ex-wife say, "Hey, I don't want to be a part of your life anymore," you don't have that control. So the issue isn't just about you . . . it's about the devastation to the family. Are you aware of what happens when a parent commits suicide? The children have a huge sense of guilt, as though it was their fault. They carry that for years and years.

*But then why don't they show you the love when you're going through the pain and the hurt?*

Frustration and immaturity. But if you really truly love them, will you do what is loving toward them? I'm talking about making the decision to say, "Yes, I've hurt them in the past, but I will do my best to stop hurting them in the future." You have a choice right now, and it's an extremely important choice. . . . Where's the gun right now?

*It's right by my side.*

I would like for you to make a godly choice right now to unload the gun. Take the bullets out.

*Okay. Can you hold on for a minute?*

I will hold.

*All right, it's unloaded.*

Take those bullets and put them in another room. Now, you said you truly love your son and daughter and even your ex-wife. A son and a daughter both want the best relationship possible with their daddy. The most difficult thing about suicide is there is no way that they can have a relationship in the future.

*But they don't want me.*

They don't want what they've had with your addiction. Every son and daughter wants the best relationship possible. With suicide you cut off all potential in the future, but more than that, you don't want to do this because you told me you really love them. Actions and addictions can be changed. You don't want to destroy your kids, do you?

*No, I don't.*

I don't think you are that self-consumed, that self-centered that you would want to inflict pain for years. So what we've got to do, then, is come up with a true solution. You've told me you want to do what God wants you to do and you know the Ten Commandments say, "Thou shalt not kill."[2] So if you really want to do what God wants you to do, you have to say, "God, I know I have felt hopeless, but I will choose to eliminate the option of suicide, no matter what."

*But Ananias and Sapphira were killed because they lied to God, and I've been a sinner.*

Death can be a consequence God chooses in that He is the author of life and death. I don't think you really want to play God. I don't think your intent is, "I'm going to take the role that God alone should have." Right now you're in such pain that you're saying, "I hate the pain. I just want to end the pain."

*I just want it over.*

I think it's the addiction you need to get over. You just don't have the plan in place to get the true solution for your addiction. Addictive behavior means: Instead of *you* being in control, the behavior has control of you. But there are thousands and thousands of people who do eventually gain control.

*I went through two treatment centers, and the addiction comes back and just nails me to the wall.*

I know it's hard, but there is hope. I've done a little math here—you said you had been an alcoholic for thirty-six years?

*Thirty-six years, yes.*

And you're forty-nine. So you were an alcoholic when you were thirteen years old.

*Yes.*

The Bible says, "If anyone is in Christ, he is a new creation; the old has gone, the new has has come" (2 Cor. 5:17). Because every authentic Christian literally has Christ in him or her, Christ is the power source for change. I'm not talking about behavior modification. Anybody can modify behavior for a period of months or even years, but Christ changes people permanently . . . from the inside out.

*I believe that.*

Is it possible you want to access the supernatural power of God but you don't have Christ on the inside causing the change? When you have *Christ in you*, you have the power of God available to overcome whatever temptation, addiction, or struggle. I'm wondering if it's possible that you don't truly have Christ *in you*. So many people have made an assumption that they have Christ when they really don't. Part of it is because they know so much intellectually that it's a camouflage keeping them from seeing that they don't have the real life of Christ.

*I see what you're saying. Just because I know the Bible and I know what God wants me to do, I think it's going to happen automatically. But that's not true.*

The Bible says I can do all things through Christ, who gives me strength. It's through His power, so you need Him on the inside. The whole issue is for us to lay down our will and say, "Lord, I want your life inside of me."

*It's like the song, "Take My Life and Let It Be."*

As 2 Corinthians 13:5 says, "Examine yourselves to see whether you are in the faith; test yourselves. Do you not realize that Christ Jesus is in you—unless, of course, you fail the test?" Tyler, I think it is valuable enough for you to pray that prayer and say, "Lord, I want You in my life, not for me to have head knowledge. I need You in my heart. I need to give You absolute control. I'm out of control and have been for years. I learned some behavior modification, but I'm not transformed."

*I've been informed but not transformed.*

Yes, yes. I'm so proud of you, Tyler, because many people are too prideful to even admit they have a need. Why don't we tell God what you've just told me, that you know you need to be transformed and you need Him to transform you?

[Tyler asked Christ to take control of his life.]

*An hour ago I was desperate, but I feel a whole lot better.*

Okay. Now the beauty is found in Ecclesiastes 9:4, which says, "Anyone who is among the living has hope." You have all the hope you need, because it is God's hope.

What a priceless privilege it was to assure Tyler that God, our Provider and Protector, is with us every moment . . . from the time storm clouds formulate until they dissipate. And what a priceless privilege it was to see authentic Christian hope birthed in Tyler's life as he grabbed hold of his Anchor.

Tyler's hand on that gun was just like my foot on that accelerator all those years ago. Despair darkened our days; we held no hope that the sun would ever break through and shine joy, peace, and unconditional love upon our lives. Hopelessness is indeed the most serious of matters; it can drive desperate people to take desperate measures, pursuing a permanent solution in an effort to end overwhelming pain.

But comprehending God's love and faithfulness and recognizing that God has a plan for our lives, people like Tyler and me, *and perhaps you*, can move forward . . . healed by hope . . . held secure by our Anchor.

## TRANSFORMATION AND AFFIRMATION

You see, when I entrusted my life to Christ, everything began to change. Hope began to illuminate my life . . . almost imperceptibly at first, then breaking forth in irrepressible light.

I wasn't the first one to notice the newly dawned light in my soul. It was my friends at Colorado summer camp. The summer after I invited Christ into my life, I was sent off to camp . . . again. Once there, others told me they noticed something different about me, about my countenance, about my attitude.

While I still wished to be elsewhere, unlike previous summers when I reluctantly and begrudgingly participated in activities, this summer I was present and I was engaged. But the strange thing about it was, I did not make a conscious decision to be different . . . I just was.

Without my even realizing it, God was changing me not only on the inside but also on the outside. Had it not been for the encouraging comments directed toward me, I don't think I would have even noticed something mysteriously wonderful happening to me.

I was unaware of hope burrowing its way into my heart and lodging itself there, hope that was being evidenced by my newfound ability to find good in my once grim camping experiences. During previous summers I'd hiked the same steep, rocky switchback trails and fished from the same fresh mountain streams; I had shot bullets and arrows at targets, paddled canoes, and ridden horses. I had done all the things summer campers do in the Colorado mountains. Yet no one could tell on the outside that on the inside I was *alone, isolated, emotionally disengaged*. I went through the motions, but it was always without emotions.

## THE SWEET SIDE OF PAIN

But now for the first time, not only was I more fully aware of the natural beauty of my surroundings, I was more acutely aware of a sensitivity to others' pain that God was developing within me.

An early manifestation of this was my reaching out to a fellow camper . . . a painfully shy loner like I had been. (I now see the sweet foreshadowing of God's call on my life to bring His hope to the hopeless through the many avenues He has afforded me.)

Clearly, the feeding I had been receiving from God's Word since my conversion, through prayer and careful study, was beginning to produce fruit in me even without my awareness. It was a result of the spiritual hunger God created in me when He took up residence within me when I become a Christian.

Back home I began literally living for Sundays, when I could sit at the feet of my fabulous Bible teacher at church and be fed spiritual food that slowly began to fill a deep, deep void in my life . . . a colossal chasm in my heart.

The truths in God's Word encouraged me to cling to the hope that even though I did not understand why God did not change my caustic father or our painful circumstances at home, I could trust Him to direct my path. During those early years with the Lord, I clung for dear life to Proverbs 3:5–6: "Trust in the LORD with all your heart and lean not on your own understanding; in all your ways acknowledge him, and he will make your paths straight."

I counted on God to be my security. I staked my life on Him. He was all I had. As a result, I began to learn one of life's most precious lessons: God is all I need. And He is the Anchor that never fails . . . even when trouble hits, wave upon wave.

> For the waves of death encompassed me,
>     the torrents of destruction assailed me;
>   the cords of Sheol entangled me;
>     the snares of death confronted me.
>   In my distress I called upon the LORD;
>     to my God I called.
>   From his temple he heard my voice,
>     and my cry came to his ears. (2 Sam. 22:5–7 ESV)

## Anchoring Your Hope: A Boat without a Rudder/A Ship without a Sail

It was a warm California day in June 2002. Richard Van Pham launched his twenty-six-foot sailboat to travel from Long Beach harbor to Catalina Island.

As evening approached, a storm whipped around him. The winds were so treacherous, they broke the mast and rudder of his boat. To his dismay, when Van Pham attempted to call for help, his radio wouldn't work and his motor wouldn't start. Unable to control his boat, he was helplessly carried away by the wind and the waves.

At age sixty-two, this Vietnamese immigrant had no idea that his three-hour sail was about to become a three-month saga that could only be described as terrifying. His intended twenty-five-mile voyage turned into a 2,500-mile journey of isolation and desperation. Because Van Pham had no other family members, no one initiated a search or filed a missing persons report.

Each day he drifted at sea. Each day he looked for land but instead saw only boundless blue water. He survived by drinking rainwater and eating sea turtles, fish, and seagulls.

Then on September 17, hoped-for rescue became reality. A Navy P-3 patrol plane on an anti-drug interdiction mission spotted the broken-down boat almost three hundred miles off the coast of Costa Rica. A nearby ship, the USS *McClusky*, plucked Van Pham from his crippled craft and took him to Guatemala. Back on solid ground, the sailor-turned-survivor finally flew back home.[3]

Memories loomed large for Van Pham when he revisited his lost-at-sea voyage. "I didn't know where I was or where to go. For months I saw nothing . . . only water, sky, and seagulls."

Like this rescued man, many of us encounter unexpected crises in our lives. Storms whip around us, and we are blown off course. Suddenly we're fighting for our lives, struggling to stay afloat. Can we have real hope of survival? Where can we find hope? Where can we turn for help?

The psalmist tells us, "They cried out to the LORD in their trouble, and he brought them out of their distress. He stilled the storm to a whisper; the waves of the sea were hushed. They were glad when it grew calm, and he guided them to their desired haven. Let them give thanks to the LORD for his unfailing love."[4]

Whatever storm you are experiencing, allow Christ to be your Anchor. He will keep you from hopelessly drifting. He will hold you both safe and secure.

# 3

# YOUR UNFAILING ANCHOR
## HOPE HOLDS YOU FIRMLY SECURE

---

### Security:
### Outmaneuvering the Enemy

---

Not being a sailor, I had never thought much about anchors . . . until I began researching the topic of hope. First I looked at all the verses in the Bible on hope, and only one had a visual attached to it. Hebrews 6:19 (ESV) says, "We have this as a sure and steadfast anchor of the soul." I soon realized that this Scripture compares Christ . . . and hope . . . to a nautical anchor. I was intrigued. God could have used any number of objects. *Why anchors?* I wondered.

Answering that question launched a fascinating treasure hunt—scouring nautical literature on the mechanics and purposes of anchors, then using my findings to draw conclusions about biblical applications.

The more I learned about anchors, the more I appreciated the marvelous similarities between the holding power of an anchor and the holding power of Christ . . . discoveries that have changed my life and, I pray, will change yours. So join me now on your own treasure hunt to discover the power of an unfailing Anchor.

## PHYSICS PHENOMENON

I'm sure you know anchors are a nautical necessity. But are you aware they're also a phenomenon of physics? An anchor weighing a mere forty-five pounds can hold a four-thousand-pound ship in place. Although winds howl and waves swell, a ship will not be carried out to sea as long as the anchor tightly grips the ocean floor. Although anchors come in various sizes and shapes, ultimately all serve one purpose for a boat or ship: "keepin' her afloat." In addition:

- Anchors are typically connected to a boat or ship by a rode, a long chain or a heavy line with a short chain. Some anchors are fastened securely to the water's flooring to hold down a large object (such as an oil rig). Other anchors are like large sheets or parachutes thrown into deep water in order to slow or stabilize a vessel.
- The English word *anchor* is a translation of a Greek word derived from the word *ankos*, which means "curve."[1] Anchors are usually curved to hook on to a solid base.
- Anchors are a symbol of the sea and represent hope and steadfast-ness. (The United States Navy often uses this emblem.)
- Anchors are often used as Christian symbols to represent Christ, who provides security for believers, holding them secure no matter how severe the storm. This symbol was especially significant to the heavily persecuted early church. Many etchings of anchors have been discovered in the catacombs of Rome, where Christians held their meetings in hiding. Threatened with death because of their faith, these committed Christians used the anchor as a disguised cross and as a marker to guide the way to their secret meetings. Located be-neath the ancient city, six hundred miles of these tomb-like burial chambers served as a place of refuge during perilous times of perse-cution. Thus the anchor, found even on some tombstones today, has become the symbol of guaranteed hope for the eternal security of true Christians.

## AN ANCHOR FOR EVERY TRIAL

Conditions at sea vary—from perfectly peaceful to the perfect storm. Over the centuries sailors have crafted numerous anchors to address the unique needs of vessels amidst a wide range of environmental conditions.

The trials of life are much the same, arriving with different levels of intensity and duration. To hold us secure, we need an unfailing anchor—one specifically sized to our capacity, adapted to our needs, and able to function flawlessly . . . every single time.

For the believer, Jesus is that Anchor. Consider now just five of the many commonly used anchors and how they reflect the miraculous, mysterious, and matchless staying power of Christ.

## #1: THE MUSHROOM ANCHOR

Mostly used for smaller craft such as rowboats and canoes—vessels not anticipating major turbulence—the mushroom anchor is the least efficient of the five types because it has no "arms."[2]

*Jesus is our anchor.* As the mushroom anchor is used for smaller watercraft, Jesus stabilizes us even as we move through the seemingly "smaller," minor problems of everyday living. He helps us stay steady with people who gossip and gripe, those who lie and are lazy, those who pout and are petty, those who annoy and are nosy. Jesus anchors us when we have frustrating friends, problems with pets, worry at work . . . and the list goes on.

*Biblical example*: Some of the disciples of Jesus who were fishermen by trade experienced the frustration of working all night, only to end up empty-handed. Knowing this, Jesus told them, "'Put out into deep water, and let down the nets for a catch.' Simon answered, 'Master, we've worked hard all night and haven't caught anything. But because you say so, I will let down the nets.'"[3] Jesus then honored their obedience by filling their nets with more fish than they could possibly hold.

*Jesus has proven Himself to be my personal "mushroom anchor"* amidst the everyday trials of life. For example, shortly after graduating from college, I was asked to direct my church's junior high division, which ministered to six hundred students. Though I had no formal preparation (only four years as a Sunday school teacher), I accepted the position . . . unaware that my most effective source of training would soon come from the "School of Hard Knocks."

Such was the case one Friday evening after a youth rally when I quietly suggested to fourteen-year-old Nancy that perhaps she could refrain from talking so much about her more sophisticated wardrobe so as not to build barriers between her friends and herself.

That same night Nancy's mother phoned me, outraged that I would advise her daughter on such matters and demanding my assurances that I would never again make such a grave mistake. "If anyone's going to correct her, I'll be the one!" she snapped.

Though I felt misunderstood, I didn't feel led to try to argue my case with Nancy's mother. As anger threatened to boil within me, God reminded me of Proverbs 15:1, "A gentle answer turns away wrath." With a softened heart, I decided to give a higher priority to the relationship with Nancy and her mother than to the satisfaction of being understood or making my point. I apologized to mother and daughter and asked for forgiveness, which ultimately enabled me to remain a part of Nancy's life.

Looking back, I see how God worked through that trial for my good, strengthening my faith and teaching me an invaluable lesson. Even if my motive is right, I can expect to be accused of doing wrong. But Jesus is there to anchor me.

## #2: THE FLUKE ANCHOR

Lightweight, but with high holding power, the fluke anchor buries itself in the watery bottom, working best in sand, mud, or clay.[4]

*Jesus is our anchor*. Like the fluke anchor, Jesus stabilizes us with a powerful hold. He is strong and steady, yet His presence brings us peace—a lightness even amidst difficult circumstances (poor choices, money problems, prodigal loved ones, painful accusations). When we struggle within ourselves and question our decisions . . . when we have unforeseen challenges and changes . . . when we doubt who we are and even doubt who *He* is, Jesus anchors us with His power and peace.

*Biblical example*: Jesus sent the disciples ahead of Him by boat to the other side of the lake so He could have time alone to pray. In the middle of the night Jesus walked toward the boat . . . on the water. Astonished, Peter instantly wanted to join Jesus on the water. Jesus said, "Come," and Peter did! He stepped out and began to walk, but then his faith was swallowed up by fear. As he took his eyes off Jesus, Peter faltered with fear, started to sink, and cried out. Jesus then reached out and rescued him.

"Lord, if it's you," Peter replied, "tell me to come to you on the water."
"Come," he said. Then Peter got down out of the boat, walked on the
water and came toward Jesus. But when he saw the wind, he was afraid
and, beginning to sink, cried out, "Lord, save me!" Immediately Jesus
reached out his hand and caught him. "You of little faith," he said, "why
did you doubt?" And when they climbed into the boat, the wind died
down. (Matt. 14:28–32)

*Jesus has proven Himself to be my personal "fluke" anchor* amidst tumultuous trials and painfully poor choices. My years as a church youth
director again come to mind. For weeks someone had been mali-
ciously placing nails on the ramps into the church parking garage. All
staff members were asked to be on the lookout for the culprit. I soon
received word that a ninth grader in my division, whom I'll call Dave
Todd, was to blame.

I really liked Dave, "all boy" that he was. But it was my job to
inform his parents of the disturbing news. Dave's mother was a kind
and well-regarded Vacation Bible School teacher at our church. It
didn't take long to locate her. After broaching the topic of Dave's mis-
conduct, I told her where the security officer was holding Dave. *If I
were a parent, I'd want to know*, I told myself.

That evening I received an irate phone call from Dave's father, a
highly influential lawyer. "How dare you talk to my wife in front of her
friend?" (To be candid, I was so focused on finding Mrs. Todd, I didn't
realize anyone else was around!) "Meet me at your office tomorrow
morning," he demanded. "And you had better be ready to make your
statements about my son stand up in court!"

Petrified, I envisioned a gut-wrenching showdown. It was that and
more. At the beginning of the early-morning conference, which lasted
three hours, I apologized to Mrs. Todd. "Sharing about Dave in front of
your friend was totally insensitive, and I am so terribly sorry," I told
her. "Would you forgive me?" She said she would.

However, the momentary relief I felt following her gracious
response was quickly overshadowed by Mr. Todd. I can truthfully say
that up to that point in my life I had never been talked to in such a
manner. He would ask a question, and as I began my answer, he would

cut me off mid-sentence with sarcastic antagonism. Over and over again I was dismissed, disregarded, disrespected.

As my mock trial continued—filled with yelling, accusations about my character, and threats to have me fired—I chose to say nothing. Instead I spoke silently to God. Soon Proverbs 16:7 began to anchor me in the Lord's unchanging truth: "When a man's ways are pleasing to the LORD, he makes even his enemies live at peace with him."

In the end I was not fired from my job. Instead I learned an important lesson: "Praise in public, confront in private." And I learned about God's surpassing greatness as a stabilizing anchor in my life.

### #3: THE PLOW ANCHOR

Plow anchors are typically massive and heavy and are often able to swivel. Versatile and adaptable, they are effective in rock, kelp, grass, weeds, sand, and mud (though not in heavy grass).[5]

*Jesus is our anchor.* Like the plow anchor, Jesus stabilizes us when all we can see around us are problems. With the plow anchor's swivel capabilities comes an agility and adeptness to anchor. Jesus anchors us even through life's most difficult circumstances—the death of a loved one or a devastating diagnosis, for example. When our problems are overwhelming and what we see saddens our soul, Jesus never fails to be our anchor.

*Biblical example*: Early in His ministry, Jesus traveled to Capernaum, where he was approached by a high-ranking Roman soldier, a centurion in charge of a hundred men. The man's beloved servant was paralyzed and in deep pain, and his only hope for relief was healing from the Son of God Himself. Jesus agreed to go to the centurion's home and heal the servant, but the centurion respectfully stopped Him. In recognition of Jesus' authority and power, he humbly professed, "Only say the word, and my servant will be healed."[6] Jesus marveled at the centurion's powerful confession of faith and said He'd seen nothing like it in all of Israel. And then He healed the suffering servant.

Then Jesus said to the centurion, "Go! It will be done just as you believed it would." And his servant was healed at that very hour. (Matt. 8:13)

*Jesus has proven Himself to be my personal "plow" anchor* amidst one of the most painful losses of my life—the death of my precious mother. In 1998 Mother was diagnosed with inoperable liver cancer. She died the following year at age eighty-three. A kinder, more humble, thoughtful, and loving woman I have never known.

Washington Irving said, "A mother is the truest friend we have, when trials heavy and sudden, fall upon us; when adversity takes the place of prosperity; when friends who rejoice with us in our sunshine desert us; when trouble thickens around us, still will she cling to us, and endeavor by her kind precepts and counsels to dissipate the clouds of darkness, and cause peace to return to our hearts."[7]

Such was the case with my mother. I don't know how it would have been possible to love another mother more than I loved her. How I treasure the incredibly precious times I shared with Mom during the last year of her life. One Sunday evening holds an especially tender place in my heart.

Ravaged by cancer, for the entire weekend Mother had no sleep—not even an hour—and she had become uncharacteristically restless, frequently trying to get out of bed, yet still hooked up to an IV tube. Meanwhile her hospice nurse was unable to comfort her.

I arrived at midnight, hoping to help. When I began singing softly to her, the music calmed her. So I slipped into bed beside her and just put my arm around her. Then she gently placed her head on my shoulder. For the first time in seventy-two hours, she was calm as I sang hymns of faith to her, along with all of her fun favorites, for six hours straight. We would often sing together, "You've Got to Accentuate the Positive."

Never will I forget the love in her eyes throughout the early morning hours, Mother gazing up at me doe-like during this musical marathon. Around 5:00 A.M. she finally drifted into a peaceful slumber.

Though I knew our time together was short, God graciously anchored my soul—my mind, will, and emotions—in the painful, yet comforting truth that one day it would be far better for Mother to be "away from the body and at home with the Lord" (2 Cor. 5:8). To all who knew her, it was evident that God's peace, favor, and comfort rested upon my mother, whose hope remained steadfastly in Him until the moment she took her last breath on earth and entered into the Savior's waiting arms.

After my mother's death, Eleanor, one of my dearest friends, confided that by watching Christ anchor me during this painful time of loss, she had rock-solid hope during her own beloved mother's homegoing that she too would be anchored by Christ.

## #4: THE CLAW ANCHOR

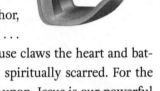

Originally designed for offshore gas and oil rigs, claw anchors are most effective on rocky, gravel, and coral bottoms.[8]

*Jesus is our anchor.* Like the claw anchor, Jesus stabilizes us when we are victimized . . . when verbal abuse, violence, or sexual abuse claws the heart and batters the body, leaving us emotionally and spiritually scarred. For the times when we feel powerless and preyed upon, Jesus is our powerful anchor, holding us strong and secure.

*Biblical example*: Jesus one day told His disciples that they would all go across to the other side of the lake. Once on the water, Jesus fell into a deep sleep and was not awakened by a powerful storm that swamped the boat. The experienced crew believed they would surely drown! In desperation they cried out to Jesus. With only a few words He calmed the storm.

> The disciples went and woke him, saying, "Master, Master, we're going to drown!" He got up and rebuked the wind and the raging waters; the storm subsided, and all was calm. "Where is your faith?" he asked his disciples. In fear and amazement they asked one another, "Who is this? He commands even the winds and the water, and they obey him." (Luke 8:24–25)

*Jesus has proven Himself to be my personal "claw" anchor during one of* the darkest times of my life—a time when a traitorous "friend" stealthily sought to sabotage our ministry . . . and me.

"Julie" came to Hope For The Heart from another highly regarded ministry. In fact, I didn't recruit her—she recruited me. "God told me I need to come help you," she announced confidently during our first conversation. I was humbled and overjoyed that our little ministry, only a few years old at the time, could attract such an experienced pro with what sounded like a stellar record of achievements. What's more, the head of our ministry had moved to Canada to follow her husband's career reassignment. *God sent Julie to me just in time,* I thought.

But six months after her arrival, odd, inexplicable things began happening around the ministry with growing regularity. Unwise expenditures were authorized with my approval . . . except I *hadn't* approved them. A key ministry relationship was terminated at my request . . . except I *hadn't* requested it. Hurtful accusations about our staff were attributed to me . . . except I *hadn't* said them.

Before my eyes, everything our team had worked so hard to build . . . including our staff's *esprit de corps*—suddenly seemed to be unmoored and drifting out to sea. I knew something was horribly wrong, yet I was unable to ascertain the source.

One day, about a year and a half after Julie's arrival, I was feeling frustrated and confused. Then after a board meeting to help other ministries, I sighed under my breath, "It's wonderful to help others, but I can't help myself."

Unknown to me, my lament had been overheard by an astute businessman who had been standing at an angle far behind me. John immediately followed up, pressing me to explain. Though embarrassed and a bit ashamed, I finally told him about the ministry's mysterious woes and how powerless I felt to stop them.

John immediately asked permission to conduct a thorough investigation, and I agreed. After three weeks he revealed his findings. "June," he bluntly said, "you have a snake in the grass, and that snake is Julie."

John presented incontrovertible evidence of Julie's fraudulent, unethical practices, corroborated by countless staff, vendors, and other colleagues with whom John had spoken, individuals reluctant to come to me because of lies they'd been told. Earlier I knew about a few little white lies; however, I had let them slide.

Armed with the truth, I terminated Julie's employment. Even after her departure, I learned more about how she had sought to pit one staff member against another.

Little by little, equilibrium began to return . . . to the ministry, to the staff, and to my life. With it came the blessed reminder that through one of the darkest storms of my life, one that threatened the very life of this ministry as none other before or since, God did, in fact, serve as my anchor, stabilizing me.

In the midst of the pain Jeremiah 29:11, the ministry's theme verse, comforted me time and again: "'I know the plans I have for you,' declares the LORD, 'plans to prosper you and not to harm you, plans to give you hope and a future.'"

Throughout this ordeal, I was given a divine opportunity to do for myself what I have counseled thousands of HOPE IN THE NIGHT callers to do: "Hold on to hope." By taking my own advice, I learned two priceless lessons: First, confront any and every breach of integrity, and second, Jesus is my Anchor, and He is holding me.

Don't give up the hope to which He has anchored you . . . hold on and keep on holding!

## #5: THE SEA ANCHOR

Made of sturdy cloth like either a giant sail or a parachute, the sea anchor is lowered into the water to create a drag and slow the vessel,  especially when water depth is too great for an anchor to grab hold of the bottom.

*Jesus is our anchor.* Like the sea anchor, Jesus stabilizes us when we feel like a ship haplessly tossed about on the water . . . out of control . . . because of a compulsive addiction or besetting sin. In the depth of our souls, He slows us down, helping us to see how our continual wrong choices will ruin our relationships and shatter our dreams. Jesus anchors us when the powerful waves of personal disappointment leave us in deep despair . . . perhaps even so much so that suicide is considered . . . something, *anything* to stop the pain. Even in the most troubling, turbulent times, Jesus is our Anchor . . . even in the darkest part of the deep.

*Biblical example*: As a prisoner facing possible death, the apostle Paul was being transported by ship to Rome to stand trial. In the midst of hurricane-strength winds, the crew lost control of the ship. The tempestuous wind tossed the ship like a weightless cork toward the shore. In an attempt to diminish their speed, they let down the *sea anchor*. This was their only hope of not crashing into sandbars at a speed that would cause certain death.

> Paul stood up before them and said: ". . . I urge you to keep up your courage, because not one of you will be lost. . . . Keep up your courage, men, for I have faith in God." (Acts 27:21–22, 25)

*Jesus has proven Himself to be my personal "sea" anchor* when life has careened off course and all hope seemed to be lost. Since giving my life to Christ, there have been times when I wanted my life to be over. Not that I wanted to kill myself—I didn't have a plan for doing so. However, at certain times my soul has been so anguished that I simply didn't care to go on living. . . . I just wanted to go *Home*.

How clearly I recall one such instance. I was sitting in my breakfast nook, contemplating one of the most painful situations I'd ever faced as a follower of Christ. Yet I remember, amidst the pain, being surprised at my perspective. My internal conversation went something like this:

"I am dreading the inevitable pain I'm about to face. However, I recognize that in the past God has used my pain to build compassion, empathy, and insight in my life. Even though I am going to hurt . . . and hurt badly . . . like all pain before it, this pain has a beginning, but it will also have an end. I am going to grow, and I am going to learn. In the process I am going to hold on to God's promises and believe that He will never fail me as I place my hope in Him. First Peter 1:6–7 will be true in my life: Now for a little while you may have had to suffer grief in all kinds of trials. These have come so that your faith—

of greater worth than gold, which perishes even though refined by fire—may be proved genuine and may result in praise, glory and honor when Jesus Christ is revealed."

I wish I could say I've approached every crisis with mature hope and faith. I have not. But what peace I have known when I have chosen, as an act of my will, to place my hope in God despite my circumstances, anchoring my future and my faith in Him! He has never failed me, and, my friend, He will never fail you.

## HIDDEN HELPERS

Have you ever been storm-tossed, in pain, and you didn't know what to do? So you said, "Lord, where are You? Why aren't You here? I don't see You helping me at all!"

Realize, although each of the five anchors are different, they share one very important characteristic: If they are doing their job, *you won't see them!* They always perform their job sight unseen. They are always invisible to those onboard . . . to those who hope they will be held tight.

You don't have to "see" anchors to know that they're working. What's going on above the surface lets you know what's going on below the surface.

But anchors stowed away in a ship's stern while storms rage can only be considered valueless, useless, powerless. They must be purposefully put to use, their intended function applied when the ship is vulnerable and unsteady, when it's capable of capsizing from tremendous environmental pressures.

## YOU HAVE BEEN GIVEN AN
## *ANCHORARIUS*

In ancient times ships had an *anchorarius*, a forerunner.[9] This sailor went before and was in charge of the ship's main anchor. The forerunner, along with other sailors, would carry the anchor inside a smaller boat and set it down in a safe harbor.

Although the huge ship remained outside the harbor, it was

anchored close to the shore. The anchor firmly held the ship against turbulent winds and waves that would otherwise push it out to sea or cause it to crash against the rocky shoreline.

Once on land, the original forerunner was the one person chosen to run to a designated place before all others, arriving for three purposes:

- to give notice of their approach,
- to take possession in their name,
- to prepare for their arrival.[10]

We also have a forerunner, a spiritual forerunner, and His name is Jesus. Following His resurrection, He led the way to heaven to prepare a place for us, ensuring that we too will be raised to live a new life in heaven.

Jesus is your *anchorarius*, your steadfast hope, your sturdy anchor, keeping you afloat when the buckling winds and battering waves slam against you. No storm is strong enough to separate you from your Almighty Anchor . . . not even an inch. Nothing is destructive enough to detach you from your Anchor. He holds you firm and secure.

This is God's promise to every authentic Christian:

> We have this hope as an anchor for the soul, firm and secure. It enters the inner sanctuary behind the curtain [heaven], where Jesus, who went before us, has entered on our behalf. (Heb. 6:19–20)

## SIX SPIRITUAL ASPECTS OF AN ANCHOR

Ultimately Jesus will lead you to your final home . . . the safe harbor of heaven. And there the storms of life will stop and be forever still.

To help you always remember that God is the only Anchor we can truly rely on and to help you clearly understand what biblical, Christian hope is, ponder the following points based on the acronym ANCHOR:

- **A**ccept Christ as your only hope. "I pray also that the eyes of your heart may be enlightened in order that you may know the hope to which he has called you" (Eph. 1:18).
- **N**ever put your hope in what is seen but in what is unseen. "In this hope we were saved. Now hope that is seen is not hope. For who hopes for what he sees? But if we hope for what we do not see, we wait for it with patience" (Rom. 8:24–25 ESV).
- **C**laim the plans God has for your future. "I know the plans I have for you, declares the LORD, 'plans to prosper you and not to harm you, plans to give you hope and a future" (Jer. 29:11).
- **H**ope in the redeeming power of God. "Why are you downcast, O my soul? Why so disturbed within me? Put your hope in God, for I will yet praise him, my Savior and my God" (Ps. 42:5–6 ).
- **O**ffer genuine faith, hope, and love to other Christians. "We always thank God, the Father of our Lord Jesus Christ, when we pray for you, because we have heard of your faith in Christ Jesus and of the love you have for all the saints—the faith and love that spring from the hope that is stored up for you in heaven" (Col. 1:3–5).
- **R**each out to others so they might know the hope of His calling. "Put your hope in the LORD, for with the LORD is unfailing love and with him is full redemption" (Ps. 130:7).

Ships at sea cannot survive severe storms without the use of anchors. And if you are anchorless on the "sea of life," neither will you survive. Traumatic tides of trouble will wash you ashore . . . beaten, battered, and bemoaning the purposelessness of it all. But with Jesus as your Anchor you not only have *peace*, you have *perspective*—that no pain is pointless, that all that happens to you is purposeful as God unfolds His perfect plan for your life.

And that perfect plan involves *storms*, according to God's infinite wisdom. But because of God's infinite love, He has provided an invincible Anchor that will never let go of you.

> He is my loving God and my fortress, my stronghold and my deliverer, my shield, in whom I take refuge. (Ps. 144:2)

# Anchoring Your Hope:
# Outmaneuvering the Enemy[11]

The USS *Constitution* sailed out of Chesapeake Bay, headed northward for New York in the early weeks of the War of 1812. Her crew was dismayed to encounter a large squadron of British warships. The fleet—including four mid-sized warships and one smaller ship—clearly had the *Constitution* outnumbered, outmanned, outgunned.

In his official report to the Secretary of the Navy, Captain Isaac Hull described the threat: "Saw two frigates . . . One within five or six miles and [four vessels] about ten to twelve miles . . . all in chase of us . . . coming up very fast."[12]

Throughout the night of July 17, the British ships sailing under the Union Jack jockeyed for position to overtake the lone vessel flying the Stars and Stripes. As the ocean breezes stilled to a dead calm, Captain Hull further documented the crisis: "It soon appeared . . . that our escape was impossible . . . and not the least hope of a breeze, to give us a chance of . . . out-sailing them."[13]

But Captain Hull soon came up with an alternative strategy to save the vessel. He would try to keep the *Constitution* out of harm's way . . . by *kedging*.

Captain Hull ordered a small boat to tow two of the *Constitution's* anchors far ahead of the ship and then drop them into the ocean. As soon as the anchors were deployed (about 2,400 feet ahead of the ship), the seamen on deck immediately began winding the rope onto the capstan, drawing the *Constitution* toward the anchors in the sea and away from the pursuing ships. The process was repeated again and again, and soon the ship slipped out of danger. However, the enemy ships, also stalled because there was no wind, copied Captain Hull's clever naval strategy.

For the next two days and nights the kedging continued. Although shots were fired, the *Constitution* steadily increased her lead, and eventually the British gave up their pursuit.

Just like the *Constitution*, you may find yourself stalled with no wind in your sails. You're in a helpless situation . . . you need to move out of harm's way. It's then that you need an Anchor not just to steady you but also to draw you away from a destructive situation . . . to draw you away from danger. As with kedging, the more you draw near to the Anchor, the more you move out of danger.

Jesus works in our lives like a kedge anchor, moving us out of harm's way, drawing us closer to Him. The spiritual rode connecting us to Him is unbreakable. We are forever attached to our Anchor as He leads us across the seas of life.

> Draw near to God, and he will draw near to you. (James. 4:8 ESV)

# 4

# THE FLASH FLOODS OF AFFLICTION

## HOPE TEACHES YOU TO TRUST

---

*Trust:*

*Caught in the Rip Current*

---

"You have cancer. You will have a mastectomy. You will lose your hair."

Those were the exact words spoken to me rapid-fire and matter-of-factly by the radiologist in October 2001. I was stunned. The whole situation seemed surreal, and the diagnosis immediately sent my thoughts spinning. *But I have to speak at a conference in Baltimore in two days and right after that in New York. I don't have time for cancer.*

*How can this be right? I have no family history of breast cancer. I've never even considered it a possibility.*

*And what does my hair have to do with this? If I have cancer and need to have a mastectomy, my hair is the least of my concerns.*

I should also point out that this diagnosis came a month after the September 11, 2001, terrorist attacks against the United States. My personal crisis occurred at almost the same time as our horrendous national crisis. Neither crisis took God by surprise . . . *that* I knew beyond a shadow of a doubt. But still I found myself longing for and needing more . . . *hope.*

## DAZED AND DISORIENTED

If you've ever been hit with sudden bad news, you know the feeling—immediate distress, disorientation, disbelief. *It just can't be.* I kept asking myself, *Can this really be happening?*

Driving home from the hospital with my assistant and dear friend Kay, we rode along in silence, both of us numb and dazed. Arriving at my house, we stood in the entryway for a moment, trying to figure out what to do next. It seemed pointless to go right back to life's mundane tasks—attending to paperwork, returning emails, checking phone messages.

Then I noticed tears in Kay's eyes. I said, "It's going to be all right, Kay. *I'll* be all right."

"I know, I know . . ." she said, and her voice trailed off.

Kay is not typically a teary person. But there she was, her eyes filling with pools of water. Aside from my deep appreciation for Kay's concern, I took her tears as another sign that I was in for a very extraordinary experience.

The following night a group of close friends gathered at my house to pray for me. These precious people all came to pray for *me*. That had never happened before. It had always been me going with a group of people to pray for someone else in crisis. Now the roles were reversed. Another surreal moment.

## HOPE IN THE MIDST OF MORE AFFLICTION

The next day, while waiting at the airport for my flight to Baltimore, my doctor called to tell me that not only did I have cancer in one breast, I had an even more aggressive type of cancer in the other one. It couldn't be felt because it was growing toward the chest wall. A third surreal moment.

From Baltimore I went on to the New York City conference. I was there to train pastors, counselors, and other caregivers on how to respond to those suffering the emotional and spiritual aftershocks of the terrorist attacks. I was both grateful and humbled by the opportunity and glad I had kept the commitment.

Besides feeling that I was doing my part to help and serve, I was clearly moved and motivated by the faith, hope, and love I found in the sad faces and broken hearts of those attending the conference.

And I was reminded once again of the ways God helps us through adversity and affliction. They were resources I would draw upon again and again through the long months of chemotherapy and recovery following surgery. It was a grueling ordeal, to be sure, but hope kept me anchored.

## ARE FAITH AND HOPE THE SAME THING?

In dealing with cancer, in submitting to God's perfect will that allowed such an occurrence in my life, there were two things I needed to exercise—faith and hope. Sometimes two words are so intertwined that it is difficult to distinguish their meanings. Such is the case with faith and hope.

Although the two concepts overlap in many ways, the Bible does differentiate between them. We know they are different, for instance, because Paul uses them in a sequence: "Now these three remain: faith, hope and love" (1 Cor. 13:13).

## DIFFERENCES BETWEEN FAITH AND HOPE

Hope is based on an assured promise, whereas faith is acting on that promise. Faith is hope put into action. Since a picture is worth a thousand words, picture in your mind a ship anchored in the water.

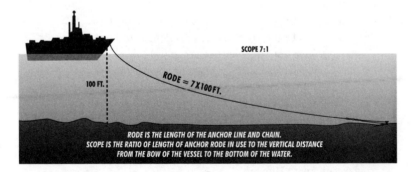

SCOPE 7:1

100 FT.

RODE = 7 X 100 FT.

RODE IS THE LENGTH OF THE ANCHOR LINE AND CHAIN.
SCOPE IS THE RATIO OF LENGTH OF ANCHOR RODE IN USE TO THE VERTICAL DISTANCE
FROM THE BOW OF THE VESSEL TO THE BOTTOM OF THE WATER.

- The water represents the sea of people and circumstances you encounter in this life.
- The ship in the water represents you as a believer safely navigating through life.
- The anchor in the water represents the guaranteed hope that Christ will hold you secure to keep you from drifting dangerously off course. Realize, when the anchor is at work, you won't see it!

- The rode is a strong chain with one end connected to the ship and the other to the anchor. In fact, the anchor holds strong and secure with a scope ratio of five to seven times farther away than the depth of the water. The rode connected to the anchor represents your faith in action . . . acting in faith that Christ will hold you secure. The act of anchoring (dropping the anchor and chain into the water) is based on the guaranteed hope that the anchor will hold.

Having hope that we can be secure is necessary for us to take the action needed to be made secure. Acting in faith is necessary so that hope is not an empty, lifeless concept but rather a living hope based upon the guaranteed promises of God, leading us to experience an anchored life.

*In physical life . . .*
- Our hope for sustaining physical life resides in believing in the benefit of food (accepting that eating food is necessary to stay alive).
- Our faith is exercised when we actually eat food for sustenance.
- If we have no hope in the merit of food, we will not eat and will prematurely die.

*In spiritual life . . .*
- Our hope in Jesus is based on the promise of God the Father that God the Son would be the Savior of the world; thus our hope is Jesus. By faith we receive Jesus into our hearts and lives; therefore, faith is the means by which we actually receive our hope.
- Our hope in Jesus prompts us to step out in faith, taking God at His word. Our faith is motivated by our hope, and faith is the means by which we benefit from our hope. Placing our faith in Jesus is the means by which we take hold of our hope in Him and receive all the benefits of having Jesus, including living an anchored life and spending eternity with Him.
- Our hope for eternal life is Jesus, because of His finished work on the cross for the forgiveness of our sins. But if we refuse to have hope *in* Him, we will spend eternity separated *from* Him.

As you sojourn on the sea of life, Christ has set you on His course, first to save you and then to conform you into His image. Having the assurance of hope is necessary before you can act in faith. Then you act in faith because of your hope. Ultimately, the Bible says that your hope is the catalyst that produces your faith.

> ... the faith and love that spring from the hope that is stored up for you in heaven and that you have already heard about in the word of truth, the gospel. (Col. 1:5)

## HAVING NO HOPE AND FAITH CAN BE FATAL

To illustrate from my own family, when my dad was in his sixties, he went to his doctor for a checkup. Tests revealed he had polyps in his colon. Knowing they could become cancerous, the doctor recommended surgery.

My dad's response? "No! All doctors want to do is cut on you." Always skeptical of physicians, he chose not to listen to the specialist. But here's the point: Because Dad didn't have hope in the medical evaluation, he didn't have faith to act upon it. Ultimately my father's refusal to believe the diagnosis and to act on the doctor's recommendation had deadly results: My dad later died of colon cancer—needlessly.

On the other hand, since I did have hope in the accuracy of my cancer diagnosis, I acted in faith, followed the recommended treatment plan, and by the grace of God survived.

## CLOCKING HURRICANE INTENSITY

The storms of life greatly vary in intensity, like the hurricanes evaluated and ranked on the Saffir-Simpson Hurricane Wind Scale. Category 1 hurricanes sustain winds from 74 to 95 miles per hour. At the other end of the scale are Category 5 hurricanes with winds measuring more than 155 miles per hour.

A Category 1 hurricane could be likened to a friend letting you down, so you have to cancel a long-anticipated trip. Circumstances are swirling around you, but you're not in danger of being blown over. A Category 5 hurricane would have to be associated with our greatest enemy, death, and could be likened to the loss of a child, spouse, or parent. Category 5 storms send us sprawling if we're not anchored . . . *anchored in Christ.*

My experience with cancer was a Category 4 hurricane: Without treatment I faced the prospect of death, but exercising hope and faith kept me anchored as I submitted to God's plan for my life.

## PAUL IN THE PERFECT STORM

A favorite motif used by the apostle Paul to explain spiritual principles could be called a nautical theme, with numerous references to storms, anchors, sailing, buffeting winds. Paul knew his readers could relate to these metaphors because much of first-century life revolved around the sea. It was a primary means of travel, it was a source of livelihood for many, and it provided much of their sustenance.

I imagine there's another reason Paul packed his writings with such imagery—personal experience. Acts chapter 27 records Paul experiencing a harrowing and hair-raising lost-at-sea drama that definitely tested his hope and faith. Paul had been arrested in Jerusalem, charged with propagating beliefs contrary to Jewish law, inciting riots, and being a ringleader of a sect.

After appealing his case all the way to Caesar, Paul was put on a ship headed to Rome with a couple hundred other people (prisoners, soldiers, and sailors). That's when things got really dicey. Almost immediately the ship ran into treacherous weather. The crew kept the vessel afloat . . . barely.

## TOSSED AND LOST AT SEA

They were tossed about on the sea like a piece of driftwood, with no chance of docking or running aground on a beach. The sailors threw cargo and tackle overboard and used all of their skills to battle one watery blast after another. After several weeks of this, all onboard believed they would die.

The entire narrative is sprinkled with phrases such as:

The wind did not allow us to go farther. . . .

Soon a tempestuous wind, called the northeaster, struck down from the land. . . .

The voyage was now dangerous. . . .

Since we were violently storm-tossed. . . . [1]

Even Paul, the stalwart man of faith, believed all was lost. He told the soldiers, "Men, I can see that our voyage is going to be disastrous and bring great loss to ship and cargo, and to our own lives also" (v. 10).

Luke, Paul's traveling companion, chronicled the event and confirmed the dire outlook: "When neither sun nor stars appeared for many days and the storm continued raging, we finally gave up all hope of being saved" (v. 20). At one point in this nautical nightmare, the crew let down not just one but four anchors. "Fearing that we would be dashed against the rocks, they dropped four anchors from the stern and prayed for daylight" (v. 29).

## THE MYSTERIOUS VISITOR

But then the ominous outlook changed with a late-night visit from an angel of God. The angel assured Paul that he would indeed testify before Caesar and that God would graciously preserve the lives of the men sailing with him. An emboldened Paul addressed his shipmates: "But now I urge you to keep up your courage, because not one of you will be lost; only the ship will be destroyed. . . . So keep up your courage, men, for I have faith in God that it will happen just as he told me" (vv. 22, 25).

After several weeks at sea, the ship's captain spotted a beach and attempted to run the ship aground. But the craft rammed into a reef instead and got stuck. The ship was then battered by the surf and broke apart. The men were forced to jump overboard and swim to shore or cling to planks as they were swept toward land. Miraculously, all were saved, just as the angel had promised.

Luke ends the narrative by saying, "And so it was that all were brought safely to land" (v. 44 ESV). As if breathing a huge sigh of relief,

Luke reemphasizes their safe passage in the very next verse: "After we were brought safely through . . ." (Acts 28:1 ESV).

## A COURSE CHARTED FROM ABOVE

All of us can relate to this story, even if we've never been violently tossed about at sea. Crises—catastrophic circumstances—crash upon us like spilling breaker waves and all but crush our hopes. Like the terrified passengers with Paul, all of us, at some time or another, have "prayed for day to come."[2] *God, please give me a ray of hope. Please shine a light on this dark situation.*

God assures us He will bring us safely through whatever storm we're currently facing. He is charting the course, and—in His time, in His way—He will lead us to the other side of our troubled waters. God is vitally interested in the well-being of His children, and He promises to provide all we need to weather tempestuous trials. The psalmist writes, "Remember your word to your servant, in which you have made me hope. This is my comfort in my affliction, that your promise gives me life" (Ps. 119:49–50 ESV).

## WHO'S IN CONTROL, NOT WHAT'S IN CONTROL

From the earliest moments of my cancer diagnosis and all the way through my recovery, I set my mind and heart on the Scripture, "It is my eager expectation and hope that I will not be at all ashamed, but that with full courage now as always Christ will be honored in my body, whether by life or by death. For to me to live is Christ, and to die is gain" (Phil. 1:20–21 ESV).

I had taught that passage years earlier but hadn't really thought about it in quite a while. When I needed it most, when life and death were very much in question, there it was, and my Anchor was set . . . solid, strong, and sure!

I also thought often of the Scriptures that tell us God knows the number of our days: "When I was woven together in the depths of the earth, your eyes saw my unformed body. All the days ordained for me were written in your book before one of them came to be" (Ps.

139:15–16). "Man's days are determined; you have decreed the number of his months and have set limits he cannot exceed" (Job 14:5). Since my days are known and numbered by God, I knew I was going to be okay whatever happened. Cancer is never sovereign over anyone's life—only *God is*. Though I make decisions that influence my health and well-being, my life is ultimately in His hands.

Although at peace with God's plan for my life, I very much wanted to beat cancer and was determined to do everything I could to live longer because I love ministering to people, I love the team at *Hope For The Heart*, I love my friends and family, and I love experiencing God in daily living.

To find the courage to face a combatant like cancer, I knew I had to have hope, the miracle-working power of hope in God.

## HOPE AND HEALTH

In fact, hope is so connected to wellness that physician and author Bernie Siegel, who has studied extensively the role our attitudes play in healing, said, "Refusal to hope is nothing more than a decision to die."[3]

I agree. Many of the struggling people I talk with seem resigned to defeat . . . and even death. Something has happened to rob them of hope, and they live as if depression, cancer, or tuberculosis is sovereign over their lives. Rather than turning to God and resting in His promises, hopelessness dogs them day in and day out.

My own oncologist, the wonderful Dr. Joyce O'Shaughnessy, who successfully guided me through my cancer treatment, said this:

> There is undoubtedly a strong connection between the body and the mind. An attitude can either dampen or amplify different therapies. Patients who know in their heart that they're going to overcome the illness, the whole treatment process is far more effective. The process is so much easier for them. There are fewer side effects, and much of daily life continues on as usual.
>
> People who know they're going to beat cancer, who have a very strong faith to rely on, stay active in their lives because this is just one episode in their lives. They have their whole lives in front of them, so they stay busier and more engaged, and look forward with anticipation.[4]

Dr. O'Shaughnessy is someone who has seen firsthand, time and time again, the vital role that hope plays in physical health and healing.

True hope is powerful medicine because it doesn't depend on what we can see, what a doctor diagnoses, what test results indicate, or any other tangible factors. It is rooted in God Himself. A full dose of hope fixes our spiritual eyes on our all-wise, all-powerful Creator with whom we have a relationship—an intimate relationship in which He is our heavenly Father and we are His sons and daughters.

Nothing comes into our lives that our Father hasn't allowed to pass through His protective hand . . . through His loving fingers. Nothing. So if that protective hand seems withdrawn for a brief moment, we must always remember there is purpose in the pain, and grace is available to get us through it. That should give us hope for our hearts.

## IS SCIENCE CATCHING UP TO FAITH?

As a young Christian physician, Dr. Harold Koenig noticed a trend among his patients that he couldn't ignore: People with hope rooted in a deep belief in God fared better during treatment than those without such hope. Predictably, conventional "wisdom" did not agree with his observations.

Plenty of studies had already appeared in medical journals to discredit any link between hope in God and physical and emotional wellness. Friends and colleagues tried to steer him away from the subject, which they regarded as a marginal field of investigation.

Thankfully, Dr. Koenig wasn't deterred. He decided to spend his career pursuing scientific evidence to support what Christians have known for centuries: Faith and hope in God are good for your health and well-being.

Eventually Dr. Koenig's passion led to his appointment as head of Duke University's Center for the Study of Religion/Spirituality and Health. Over the years he has overseen more than fifty compelling research projects that have led to dozens of articles published in peer-reviewed medical journals. Here are a few of the Center's findings:

- People who regularly attend church, pray, and read the Bible have significantly lower diastolic blood pressure than the less religious.

- Those who attend church regularly are hospitalized much less often than people who never or rarely participate in religious services.
- People with strong religious faith are less likely to suffer depression from stressful life events, and if they do, they are more likely to recover from depression than those who are less religious.
- Religious people live longer. A growing body of research shows that religious people are both physically healthier into later life and live longer than their nonreligious counterparts. Religious faith appears to help protect the elderly from the two major afflictions of later life: cardiovascular disease and cancer.[5]

We could fill several pages with similar findings. The anchor of hope in God's infinite love and healing power is the common denominator in all these groundbreaking discoveries. However, those without that anchor of hope can sadly be swallowed up by disease and depression. Dr. Koenig concludes:

> When the inevitable stress of daily problems—illness, financial worries, personal conflicts—threatens to overwhelm religious people, they draw on a reserve of energy and motivation that allows them to persevere. They trust God to fill the gap between what they could normally endure and what is actually required of them. They do not struggle alone, but rather see God as their active partner in the continuous struggle to achieve peace and balance in their lives.[6]

God is eager and ready to play His part. Hope assures us that we are not in this alone!

## WHEN GOD SAYS NO

When Jesus walked on the earth He performed countless miracles, including healing people from diseases. God is still very much in the business of miraculous healing, and countless lives today can give testimony to that.

But when it comes to God's plan for our personal lives, when we plead and petition for physical healing, we must remember that sometimes God's answer is *no*. For many it isn't a matter of a weak faith or divine discipline for sin, it's simply a part of the uniquely crafted plan God has created for individual lives.

I don't know why God says *yes* to healing for some people and *no* to others, but I do know He said, "As the heavens are higher than the earth, so are my ways higher than your ways and my thoughts than your thoughts" (Isa. 55:9).

Our hope must be in *Him*, that He is unfolding a plan that involves purpose in our pain. We are called to trust . . . *period*.

## GOD WALKS WITH US EVERY STEP

Because God became man in the person of Jesus, He can relate to and sympathize with all of our struggles and sorrows. As the writer of Hebrews tells us, "We do not have a high priest who is unable to sympathize with our weaknesses, but we have one who has been tempted in every way, just as we are—yet was without sin. Let us then approach the throne of grace with confidence, so that we may receive mercy and find grace to help us in our time of need" (Heb. 4:15–16).

Timothy Keller, pastor of Redeemer Presbyterian Church in Manhattan, writes, "Christianity does not so much offer solutions to the problems of suffering, but rather provides the promise of God, who is completely present with us in suffering. Only Christians believe in a God who says, 'Here I am alongside you. I have experienced the same suffering you have. I know what it is like.' No other religion even begins to offer that assurance."

Pastor Keller's church is not far from the site of the World Trade Center tragedy, and about eight hundred new people began attending his church after the disaster. The sudden influx of people pressed the question, "What does your God have to offer me at a time like this?"

Pastor Keller shared with them, "Christianity is the only faith that tells you God lost a child in an act of violent injustice. Christianity is the only religion that tells you, therefore, God suffered as you have suffered."[7]

## GOD SENDS RESOURCES TO HELP US COPE

When tragedy strikes, taking the wind out of our sails, when gales of grief threaten to blow us over, we *need* the support and love of others.

Even now, years after my battle with cancer, I am awed and amazed at the way people rallied around me.

Eleanor, Barbara, June, and Kay became my *hope angels*, accompanying me to appointments, double-checking my meds, and helping in a myriad of other ways. Meanwhile, Diane, Cheryl, Randy and Lana, Rita and Tom, and other dear ones became *hope helpers*.

Friends dropped off meals, had prayer times, and sent special cards. My niece Kimberly flew in from Seattle for ten days of help and support. My siblings spent time with me and pitched in to help. On and on it went. Having lived through the cancer experience, having so many walk with me through it, I can't imagine how I could've done it alone.

God has designed His family to love, support, and encourage one another. When we speak about God supplying hope for us, He often does it by giving us the care and compassion of others.

## GOD USES OUR PAIN FOR HIS PURPOSES

The flash floods of affliction wash over all of us. The question is, how will you and I respond? No one invites or enjoys misfortune and misery in his or her life. I wouldn't have put my signature on a sign-up sheet for cancer. But once we find ourselves in a difficult situation, we have a choice: resist God or rest in God. We can react with bitterness and anger and ultimately blame God, or we can react with hope and perseverance and ultimately trust God. Remember the promise of Romans 8:28: "We know that in all things God works for the good of those who love him, who have been called according to his purpose."

It's been said that pain is a much better teacher than pleasure. The truth is, God uses the flash floods of affliction to teach us to swim in His strength, to build Christlike character, and to bear ever more spiritual fruit.

It's challenging to remember these things when the floodwaters rise, but when they recede, we can say along with Paul, "We also rejoice in our sufferings, because we know that suffering produces perseverance; perseverance, character; and character, hope. And hope does not disappoint us, because God has poured out his love into our hearts by the Holy Spirit, whom he has given us" (Rom. 5:3–5).

Hardship can serve another purpose: It can be a powerful encouragement and witness to other people as they watch you submit to the sovereign hand of God. When diagnosed with cancer, it's easy to give in to self-pity, to become inward-focused.

Instead I prayed, "God, give me the grace and strength to use this situation to point others to You. For everyone I come in contact with and for everyone who hears my story, may they see Your power, love, and compassion in action." He answered my prayers. I've had the opportunity to share Christ with many people I would otherwise have never encountered. God is trustworthy!

# Anchoring Your Hope:
## Caught in the Rip Current

In the Hawaiian Islands, a beach called Hanakapi'ai is located on the coast of Kauai. Here jagged volcanic mountains covered in lush tropical foliage rise from the blue Pacific Ocean, but powerful ocean currents also flow immediately offshore due to the absence of protective barrier reefs.

Over the years these currents have shaped the beach and mountains into breathtaking landscapes that adorn gift books, travel guides, and postcards. In winter the sand disappears from the shore, carried away by the water. In spring the sandy beach returns.

Imagine that on a summer day you are hiking in the tropical heat for miles through the rugged volcanic terrain. Then at last you come upon the beautiful water at Hanakapi'ai Beach. It looks irresistible!

Of course you see the signs posted on the trail: "Do not go near the water! Unseen currents have killed many visitors." Obviously those unwise tourists made the mistake of swimming in bad weather. But today there's not a cloud in the sky! You clearly see the calm pools of water that are far from the churning waves. Eager to feel refreshed by a short swim, you rush toward the water's edge and run in.

Suddenly you are knocked off your feet and pulled away from shore. You've just come into direct contact with a rip current, a narrow, powerful current of water that is pulling you out to sea. Typically "rips" measure less than thirty feet wide. But this superhighway of rapid water can extend from two hundred to twenty-five hundred feet.

Do you wonder why rip currents even form? Picture the wind and waves pushing water inland on your right and left sides as you are standing in the shallow waters. Obviously the water must flow back out.

In front of you is a long sandbar running parallel to the beach that has a large section missing, and in that section is the rip current. That "rip" allows the currents coming toward you from both sides to push straight back out . . . and also to drag you out at top speed! On the surface of a rip current, the water appears calm and inviting, but below the surface the water flow is like a rapid river surging toward the open ocean. Even if you are an Olympic swimmer, you physically cannot swim back to shore against it. Instead you must turn out of it by swimming parallel to the coast and then swim to shore.

By not believing those clear words of warning, your life is endangered. If you survive, you are fortunate, and you will never forget to take a written warning seriously—it can be a matter of life and death. The Bible says, "We must pay more careful attention, therefore, to what we have heard, so that we do not drift away."[8]

Let's be honest: We've all done it! We have all ignored clear warnings found in God's Word and walked into water that looked harmless. We trusted our *own* eyes and our *own* knowledge and not God's truth. We didn't want to believe that warning applied to us.

Life is full of precarious unseen currents that can pull us swiftly away from God's perfect will. That's why it's vital to first see what the Lord says and then to take His words seriously. He knows what lies beneath. He sees the currents we cannot see. He will chart our course.

As long as your hope is anchored in the Lord, you will not drown. He will guide you from harm, teach you His truth, and give you His hope. Just as David prayed, you, too, can pray:

> Guide me in your truth and teach me, for you are God my Savior, and my hope is in you all day long. (Ps. 25:5)

# 5

## THE TIDAL WAVES OF TROUBLE

### HOPE ARMS YOU FOR ADVERSITY

*Trials:*
*Anchored in Iceberg Alley*

Few places on earth depict the story of early Christians and the struggles they faced more than the dusty catacombs beneath modern-day Rome. Take a journey back in time and picture yourself there in those beginning days of persecution and hardship. You leave the bright light of day to enter a maze of dark tunnels and cramped chambers carved into soft bedrock.

You've come here with other believers, outlaws under the watchful eye of Roman authorities, to say good-bye to one of your beloved—and brutally martyred—friends. The stale air is heavy with the odors of death and dank earth.

Your fear grows more intense with each step. Keenly aware that without warning soldiers could suddenly appear from out of the shadows and arrest you, you wonder whether you might be the next one carried sorrowfully into these tombs. What horrors might you suffer before you die? Are you strong enough to endure them?

Just when you fear that terror and despair may overwhelm you, your roving eyes spot a few symbols carved into the stone walls around you. The image of a fish reminds you that Jesus Himself was persecuted and killed by His enemies; a dove brings to mind the Holy Spirit's constant, comforting presence in your life.

## THE SAVIOR'S SYMBOL

Then suddenly you see another symbol etched deep into the arch-way just above your head. This one impacts you the most. This one takes you out of the present stench of suffering and death and trans-ports you into the future glory awaiting you in heaven. This symbol reminds you not only that Jesus suffered and died, but also how He was able to endure it.

The words burn into your mind: "Let us fix our eyes on Jesus, the author and perfecter of our faith, who for the joy set before him endured the cross, scorning its shame, and sat down at the right hand of the throne of God. Consider him who endured such opposition from sinful men, so that you will not grow weary and lose heart" (Heb. 12:2–3).

"Let us fix our eyes on Jesus . . . who for the joy set before him endured the cross." Again and again the words echo in your mind. Jesus wasn't focused on His circumstances but on His hope . . . on the guaranteed joy of being in heaven with the Father.

What did you see on that archway? What was able to so amply strengthen your resolve? You saw the image of an *anchor.* Someone walked this way before and left a message to encourage you: "There is hope. . . . Your story will not end here in these dark catacombs. . . . This will not be the final chapter. . . . God will hold you steady in the storm and see you all the way through it to heaven. Have courage! Have hope! Your anchor holds!"

When persecuted Christians took time to carve images of anchors into the stone of the catacombs, it was not just a way of affirming their belief that despite appearances they were not adrift. *They were trying to encourage those who would follow in their footsteps.*

## THE TRUTH ABOUT TRIALS

Yes, a sustained, terrifying "storm" raged all around them, but they had a powerful anchor that enabled them to focus not on their physi-cal plight but on their spiritual supply . . . not on their temporal situ-ation but on their eternal destiny . . . not on themselves but on their witness to a dying world.

Wind and waves howled, but God's people were steadied by something indestructible. And that something was hope, from which sprang forth courage.

Today those same symbols—the fish, the dove, and the anchor—are still around . . . on key chains, car bumpers, Bible covers, coffee mugs. Yet we barely notice them, much less find in them an inspiring source of hope. What has changed?

Do we trust God less? Do we need Him less? Are faith-testing times a thing of the past?

Certainly not, but you might not know it by looking at the relative comfort in which we live. The danger in great abundance is thinking, *This is how life should be.* Unlike our ancestors who patiently waited for lulls between storms, we all too often expect the sea to be storm-free.

An attitude of *entitlement* misleads many into thinking that hope in God always results in *relief* from trials when it more often gives us *courage* to endure our trials. As much as we resist the idea, it's not always in our best interest to anesthetize our pain or avoid trials.

## AN UPSIDE-DOWN WORLD

A woman named Linda called me on *Hope In The Night* because she had begun to lose hope in the face of intense suffering and injustice. Here are her comments and my response:

> *One thing I've noticed all my life is that mean-spirited people seem on top of the world. . . . . Everything seems to go their way. Then you see God-fearing, good-hearted people who would give the shirt off their back have one misfortune after another.*
>
> *It seems it doesn't matter whether you're a good person or not. I counsel, and I'm confronted with suffering all the time. I have felt hopelessness. I have cynicism. What can I impart to others? How can I encourage them? How can I help myself and help bring others out of hopelessness?*
>
> First of all I would deal with the issue of God's perspective and God's involvement in the lives of those yielded to Him. Our God is a God of hope. If I use "hope" in our common vernacular it means an optimistic desire that something will be fulfilled, but it's subject to change.

The biblical meaning of hope is very different . . . an optimistic desire with an assurance of fulfillment. It's absolutely *assured.* If God tells us there is hope in a particular area of our lives, we can go to the bank with it! The word *hopelessness* is absolute despair of having any expectation of good or of success.

*Right.*

But when you yield your will to the Lord, Hebrews 6:19 says, "We have this hope as an anchor for the soul, firm and secure." Biblical hope is not just a distant desire, hope is not a feeling, but rather it's a gift from God. Hope is His anchor for our souls that He has already thrown out upon the sea of life, to stabilize our hearts and lives.

*If in the ring you knock a boxer down enough times, he just can't get back up. What can you do to keep people from getting to that brink?*

We have Jesus as the Anchor for our souls and an example for our lives. He was hit with everything His enemies could throw at Him. He was berated, betrayed, and brutalized, but He was never without hope. If we are to be Christlike, we, too, are going to be persecuted. What we *can* do in the midst of that persecution is: Make a difference in our own personal world . . . be instruments of His love and His grace . . . and thereby change hearts and lives.

Here's the bottom line: Before we can let hope fill our hearts with courage, it's necessary to remember why we need hope in the first place. So let's talk about storms.

## "NOTHIN' BUT BLUE SKIES . . . "

When average Americans reach age sixty-five, they will have seen two million commercials on television.[1] *Two million!* The predominant message in those advertisements is, "All you need is the right *stuff* to make your troubles disappear (car, clothes, house, hot tub, retirement account). Life is meant to be one long vacation. You deserve nothing less."

And we want this stuff *now* . . . not *after* we've worked hard and sacrificed. The collective credit card debt in the United States alone is testimony to that.

Ask young people about their generation's top life goals and the answer is clear and resounding: They want to be rich and famous. . . . 81% of 18–25 year-olds surveyed in a Pew Research Center poll said getting rich is their generation's most important or second-most-important life goal; 51% said the same about being famous.[2]

Clearly, our secular society has driven home the message that fame and wealth are not only desirable above all else, but they're God-given rights. Television advertisements present life as one smooth sail . . . *until reality hits.* Troublesome times and turbulent storms quickly drown out such superficial media portrayals.

What TV commercials don't show is that there is far more "want" in the world than "plenty," and storms of all kinds have devastated millions of lives.

## HEAVENLY PURSUITS

When it comes to life pursuits, Jesus paints an entirely different picture. What is the greatest commandment? "You shall love the Lord your God with all your heart and with all your soul and with all your mind. This is the great and first commandment. And a second is like it: You shall love your neighbor as yourself" (Matt. 22:37–39 ESV). Concerning the most important pursuits in life, Jesus tells us to love God and to love our neighbor. The world tells us to love money and to love fame.

The irony is, young people today are even less likely than their parents to attain the wealth and fame they seek.

> Monetary realities are far bleaker for this generation than what their parents experienced. . . . These young people may well be dreaming when they envision futures filled with money and fame.[3]

In fact, all of us are "dreaming" when we put our hope in a life without trouble, tribulation, or sacrifice. We want to be rich and famous in order to finance or finagle our way out of storms. Christians often think that way too. We hope that becoming a believer will give us a "get out of trouble free" card. Who needs courage when we can simply escape into comfort and ease?

In Psalm 23 we eagerly read, "Surely goodness and mercy shall follow me all the days of my life" (v. 6 ESV) without considering the courage it takes to "walk through the valley of the shadow of death"

(v. 4 ESV), trusting in God's purposes, relying on His strength, learning huge life lessons through hardship.

Although the world turns a blind eye, consider the following two aspects about life's storms.

## STORMS ARE INEVITABLE

The truth is, life is *not* easy. At the same time, some lessons in life can only be learned the hard way, for it's through the fire that true character is forged. Even Jesus, the perfect Son of God, suffered for the purposes of maturing and proving. "Although he was a son, he learned obedience from what he suffered" (Heb. 5:8).

And because Jesus suffered, "We do not have a high priest who is unable to sympathize with our weaknesses" (Heb. 4:15), but rather we have a High Priest who not only prays for us but who anchors us when storms come.

When we spend our time believing that we should have nothing but blue skies, we are dangerously unprepared when storm clouds gather. We try to deny or outrun bad weather, but when it is unavoidable, we should face the storm, drop anchor, and courageously hang on to hope.

And we must never forget we are not alone or ill-equipped to face the storm. "His divine power has given us everything we need for life and godliness through our knowledge of him who called us by his own glory and goodness" (2 Pet. 1:3).

## STORMS ARE NECESSARY

All the virtues—what Paul called the fruit of the Spirit ("love, joy, peace, patience, kindness, goodness, faithfulness, gentleness, and self-control," Gal. 5:22-23)—are only lofty concepts until they've been tested under fire.

How can we build up courage without being afraid? How can we develop perseverance without being weary? How can we become merciful without being wronged? And how can we come to trust everything to God's steadfast love unless it seems our very lives depend on it?

## CALLED TO DUTY AND ALMOST DEATH

At the intersection between hardship and hope stands a present-day hero. Sam Johnson grew up in Dallas, Texas, and began a twenty-nine-year career in the U.S. Air Force at age twenty.[4] He eventually served as Director of the Air Force Fighter Weapons School ("Top Gun"). During the Korean War, Sam flew sixty-two combat missions and named his F-86 *Shirley's Texas Tornado* after his wife Shirley.

Returning to the United States, Sam flew with the world-renowned Air Force Thunderbirds precision flying team. But as the Vietnam War intensified, Sam was called back into active duty.

On April 16, 1966, during his second tour of duty, Sam was flying his twenty-fifth combat mission in his F-4 Phantom when a barrage of enemy fire sent his plane spiraling downward over North Vietnam. He survived the impact but suffered a broken arm, dislocated left shoulder, and broken back—injuries his captors exploited in their constant efforts to gain information from him.

## LEG STOCKS AND LONGTIME PERSECUTION

Sam spent nearly seven years as a prisoner of war, including forty-two months in solitary confinement. Held in the infamous Hanoi Hilton, he spent seventy-two days in leg stocks. When that torture ended, he was forced into leg irons for two and a half years. Weighing two hundred pounds when shot down, Sam shrank to around one hundred and twenty pounds, barely surviving on the occasional "meal" of weeds, pig fat, white rice, or pumpkin soup.

Sam became part of a group of eleven prisoners known as "the Alcatraz Gang." Separated from other POWs, these men were placed in solitary confinement for courageously resisting their captors' efforts to extract information through torture and other means.

"Alcatraz" was a special facility in a courtyard behind the North Vietnamese Ministry of National Defense. The men were kept in separate 3 x 9 foot cells. Each had a bare light bulb that burned around the clock to disrupt sleeping. The prisoners were locked in irons each night.

But Sam was not the only hero in his family. His wife spent two years wondering whether her husband was alive or dead, another two years without any contact from him, and still another three years worrying whether he would make it home at all. Throughout, Shirley kept her household together and raised their three children as a "single" parent.

## A REAL PATRIOT'S RETURN

Finally, on February 14, 1973, Sam returned home to the country he loved, fought for, and suffered so sacrificially to protect. His family waited anxiously as he spoke to the press and then raced to greet him, to touch him, to look into his eyes, to wrap their arms around him.

His children—Bob, Gini, and Beverly—allowed Shirley the first embrace. A few moments later, the three grown children (ages twenty-one, nineteen, and sixteen) surrounded and enveloped in their arms the father they had not seen since they were fourteen, twelve, and nine.

After his distinguished military career as a war hero and decorated combat veteran who was awarded two Purple Hearts and two Silver Stars, Sam accepted another leadership challenge. In 1991 he was elected to the U.S. House of Representatives, known among his colleagues and constituents as a man of deep conviction and faith.

## OPENING A FLOODGATE OF PAIN

Along with a delegation of U.S. legislators, Sam later returned to the place of his seven-year captivity. Although three decades had passed, horrific memories came flooding back during the hour-long tour of the prison . . . the shackles, the cramped cells, the coded taps that kept the POWs sane.

Yet in spite of the monstrous treatment he had received, Sam heard no apologies or acknowledgment of his POW status during meetings with top Vietnamese officials.

Shirley said the sight of a mannequin shackled to a bed in a way that made standing impossible caused her to weep, envisioning her husband in such a position for months on end.

"It was much more stark and depressing than anything I could think of," she said. "He said many times that the Lord was with him all the way through, and I'm sure he was, because I don't know how you could get through it without having a strong faith."[5]

## COMRADES AND CHRIST

Asked how he survived such cruel and inhumane treatment for so many years, Sam points to two things—his comrades and his Christian faith. He recites his favorite Scripture: "He gives strength to the weary and increases the power of the weak. Even youths grow tired and weary, and young men stumble and fall; but those who hope in the LORD will renew their strength. They will soar . . . like eagles; they will run and not grow weary, they will walk and not be faint" (Isa. 40:29–31).

Through all the torture during captivity, through all the harrowing experiences of flying combat missions, and through all the frustrations of wrangling over congressional legislation, Sam has never failed to give credit to God for providing him needed hope and courage.

As Sam Johnson knows all too well, hardship, fear, and pain—all part of life's inevitable storms—should prompt us to reach out and grasp that solitary Anchor that holds us like no other can.

Jesus was Sam Johnson's anchor for his soul when his body was battered beyond measure. When Sam's emotions churned like crashing waves, Jesus brought peace and power to withstand the mental affronts continually bombarding his mind.

To know joy in life, to glean all God desires for us in the midst of hurricane-sized trouble, we must face the storm. To do that, we need the steadfast anchor of God's hope to hold us. His strength keeps us steady and strong, sturdy and ever-standing.

The deepest trials or the deepest failures in your life cannot thwart God's faithfulness to you. Do you know the genuine goodness of God in your life—His immense mercy, His constant compassion, His everlasting love? He will be faithful to you forever. Do you know how to experience such a hope that will anchor you through any storm? Repeatedly say when you are in the midst of the storm, "I will hope in him" (Lam. 3:24 ESV).

**(Lamentations 3:19–25)**

**How to Put Your Hope in Him**

LOOK at the situation accurately ............................................... (vv. 19–20)

> *I remember my affliction and my wandering, the bitterness and the gall.*
> *I well remember them, and my soul is downcast within me.*

LINE up your thinking with what gives you hope ......................... (v. 21)

> *Yet this I call to mind and therefore I have hope:*

LEARN what gives hope in the midst of this situation .................. (v. 22)

> *Because of the LORD's great love we are not consumed,*
> *for his compassions never fail.*

LINGER on this fact: Every day God will be faithful to you ......... (v. 23)

> *They are new every morning; great is your faithfulness.*

LET the Lord fulfill you totally, not just partially .......................... (v. 24)

> *I say to myself, "The LORD is my portion; therefore I will wait for him."*

LEAN on this truth to receive hope for your heart ....................... (v. 25)

> *The LORD is good to those whose hope is in him,*
> *to the one who seeks him.*

# Anchoring Your Hope:
## Anchored in "Iceberg Alley"

"Everybody's lost hope," confessed Councilman Jay LaFont of Grand Isle, Louisiana, following the worst environmental catastrophe in United States history. On April 20, 2010, BP's Deepwater Horizon drilling rig exploded off Louisiana's coast, killing eleven people. The mile-deep well then began spewing millions of gallons of oil into the Gulf of Mexico . . . unchecked for months . . . closing the area's beaches and crippling its fishing industry. "As long as you have something to look forward to, a little glimmer of hope, you can move on," LaFont told reporters. "But this just drained everything out of us."[6]

Fortunately, the scenario couldn't be more different for individuals living near . . . and working on . . . the oil platform Hibernia off the coast of St. John's, Newfoundland, Canada. Residents and workers there are filled with hope, aware of the enormous amount of time and resources invested to build a structure that is said to be virtually indestructible.

The Hibernia's meticulous design incorporates a GBS (gravity-based structure) system that anchors it to the North Atlantic seabed two hundred and sixty-five feet below the water. The total structure from the ocean floor to the top of the derrick is 738 feet high, with construction costs of over six billion dollars.

Simply stated, the structure is *immovable*. It has to be! It sits in the middle of "iceberg alley," where icebergs can be as large as ocean liners. Sixteen huge concrete "teeth" surround the Hibernia. These teeth were expensive additions, designed to distribute the force of an iceberg over the entire structure and into the seabed, should one ever get close.

Radio operators plot and monitor all icebergs within twenty-seven miles of the oil rig. Any icebergs that come close are "lassoed" and towed away from the platform by powerful supply ships. Smaller bergs are simply diverted by using the ship's propeller wash or high-pressure water cannons. As rugged and as strong as this platform is, and as prepared as it is for icebergs to strike, the owners have no intention of allowing an iceberg anywhere near Hibernia.

But if something unpreventable comes its way, the Hibernia is anchored, rooted, and ready. Built to withstand a million-ton iceberg, designers claim it can actually withstand a six-million-ton iceberg, and even then it will still be functional. (Statistics indicate that a million-ton iceberg occurs only once every five hundred years, and supposedly one as large as six million tons comes around once every ten thousand years.[7])

As sturdy and secure as the massive Hibernia is, know that you have a source of protection that far exceeds any defense built by human hands. When storms rage in your life, the Lord Himself is your Anchor . . . your staunch and steady hope. When trouble like a massive iceberg threatens you, remember this: Because Jesus is your Anchor, He will give you *an anchored life*.

He is your help and your hope. He will sustain you, and He will hold you . . . safe and secure. The Bible promises:

> You will be secure, because there is *hope*;
> you will look about you and take your rest in safety. (Job 11:18)

PART TWO

# The Sources of
# Hope — Guaranteed

# 6

# TRUST IN THE CAPTAIN'S COURSE

## HOPE IN THE SOVEREIGNTY OF GOD

---

*The Sovereignty of God:*
*Keeping an Even Keel*

---

Two tiny Korean orphans—sisters, ages three and six—stepped through the door of their new home. The towering apartment building must have seemed like an enchanted palace.

They still had on the plain, threadbare clothes they'd worn at the orphanage. Their close-cropped haircuts were identical and utilitarian. The girls held hands as they walked cautiously into their new world.

"It wasn't how they were dressed that identified them as lost kids," said my friend John. "It was the wary, guarded look in their eyes. They clearly expected something bad to happen any minute."

John was an American businessman who spoke fluent Korean, a rarity among Western foreigners living there. He'd been asked by Barbara and Lamar, a couple from his church, to be present when they brought home their newly adopted daughters. The parents spoke little Korean and feared the girls would not fully understand they had a new and permanent home now.

At lunchtime Barbara served soup, sandwiches, applesauce, and glasses of cold milk. Lamar started to say grace when both girls immediately seized the milk and drank it down without stopping. Then, as the astonished adults looked on, they ate everything on their plates as fast as they could.

"It nearly broke my heart," John recounted. "Every crumb was gone in about three minutes."

Talking with the girls, John learned that children at the orphanage never hesitated to eat any food they were given or someone else would take it. In *that* world you looked out for yourself or got left behind. Insecurity was a way of life.

Over the next few months a physical transformation took place in the beautiful young sisters. Their hair grew out, and Barbara styled it with curls and ribbons. Each received a new wardrobe to replace their shabby orphanage uniforms. They had soft beds and toys of their own for the first time ever. No girls were ever more cared for than these two.

Even so, the shadow of fear that followed them through the door that day was not dispelled quickly. Trust doesn't come naturally to children conditioned to expect only hardship and lack. Several years passed before they fully accepted the love, protection, and provision that were theirs.

"Barbara and Lamar had to patiently establish two things that come relatively easily to most conscientious parents," John explained. "They had to prove that they *could* keep their promises and that they always *would* keep them."

Clearly the girls reserved their hope in a brighter future until they were sure their new parents would not let them down, as so many other people had.

## TOO JADED TO TRUST

This story reminds me what it's like for people who embark on a new life with God, freshly adopted into His family through faith in Jesus Christ. Often we walk through the doors of Christianity with that same sense of uncertainty: Does God *really* care about me? Will He always keep His promises to me?

It is simply an incredible concept that the sovereign God of the universe invites us to trust Him with *everything*. Nothing is so big, or small for that matter, that it doesn't matter to Him if it matters to us.

Just like the precious Korean girls, totally dependent on their adopted parents to meet all of their needs, we are totally dependent on God to meet all of our needs. And He is faithful . . . eager to help and to provide, eager to fill the deepest holes in our soul, eager to be the Captain of our ship.

But when people let us down or we see trust abused, we tend to hold back even when it comes to trusting God. People who grew up in house-holds where parents were not trustworthy, particularly father figures, often ascribe those marred characteristics to our perfect heavenly Father.

They have a jaded perception of what He's really like. Sometimes it can take years for their deep emotional wounds to be healed by the sound counsel of God's Word.

Psalm 27:10 assures us: "Though my father and mother forsake me, the LORD will receive me." All those abandoned by their earthly fathers are indeed not fatherless. Psalm 68:5 consoles, "A father to the fatherless . . . is God in his holy dwelling."

Trust is foundational for the strongest friendships. In fact, trust is the foundation on which the most stable, the most solid, the most secure relationships are built.[1] Thus, to enjoy God fully, we must trust God fully.

Like deists who espouse that God created the world and then withdrew from further involvement, we can find ourselves perceiv-ing God like an absentee father, a distant landlord. Sure, He invites us to live in His house, but we doubt His ability or His willingness to be involved in every facet of our everyday lives. And that ultimately means we doubt His sovereignty.

## CAPTAIN OF THE UNIVERSE

In reality, God is the active, all-knowing, all-powerful, and infallible Captain of the universe . . . and the Captain of our individual lives, when we invite His leadership.

The word *captain* comes from the Latin *caput*, meaning "head."[2] In Roman times a ship captain was known as *Magister Navis*, referring to his maximum authority aboard his vessel. Traditionally a distinctive laurel wreath adorned his head; hence the gold laurel insignia found even today on the hats of many seafaring captains.

As in centuries past, a captain has ultimate responsibility and authority for his vessel. All those aboard are subject to his command. He alone is sovereign.[3]

So it is with those who look to the heavenly Father to captain their lives. He is faithful to guide us, protect us, and provide for our every need.

There is an amazing promise describing God as our "need-meeter" in the book of Philippians: "My God will meet all your needs according to his glorious riches in Christ Jesus" (4:19). Did you catch that key word? *All* your needs . . . physical, emotional, spiritual. His resources are abundant; they never run out.

God is sovereign over your life, able to faithfully meet every need, and He wants you to live out your days with the peace and joy that come from embracing that truth. Don't be fearful . . . be faithful because our God, who abounds with love for us, can be fully trusted.

Some who reject God's sovereign provision wrongly believe, "I am the master of my fate: I am the captain of my soul.[4] My hope is in myself. My confidence is in my ability to take charge of my life and make it what I want it to be. My future is in my hands."

However, those who trust in God's sovereign provision rightly believe, "My hope is in my unchanging relationship with Jesus, my Lord and Savior, not on anything that can be taken away from me, including my own abilities and resources. He is the One who meets all of my needs . . . my Captain. In Him I have found the hope I need to embrace this present life and to anticipate my future life in heaven."

The Bible affirms, "The LORD is good to those whose hope is in him, to the one who seeks him" (Lam. 3:25).

## HOPE FOR REGAINED TRUST

J. D. is an American in his late fifties, but he shares a connection with the young Korean orphans mentioned earlier. All his life he has struggled with trust issues—trusting God, trusting other people. When J. D. was just five years old, his stepmother locked him alone in a room where her deceased mother lay in a coffin. She refused to let him out despite his desperate screams.

J. D. called Hope In The Night because more than forty-five years later he began having troubling nightmares about the incident.

J. D.'s relationship with both his parents was abusive. Provoked by the stepmother, his father would often beat him, utilizing any "weapon" at his disposal. J. D. was once hit on the back of his head with a pipe, sending him to the hospital and ultimately to the streets. He simply couldn't take any more, and J. D.'s parents couldn't have cared less where he laid his head at night.

J. D. nonetheless saw his stepmother and father occasionally, and he discovered something that brought a trickle of love his direction. If J. D. brought them something, he could usually count on a smile and a few kind words. But soon it would be over, and dysfunction would again dominate.

Over time a clear and tragic message was communicated to J. D. that has tarnished his relationships ever since: Love is gained *conditionally.* You must give to hope to get.

I asked J. D. if his abusive childhood had affected his relationship with God.

*To be honest, yes, ma'am . . . I have had difficulty trusting anyone.*

The reason I asked is, children typically ascribe to God the characteristics of their authority figures. Since your father and stepmother were not trustworthy, it follows that you would think that God is untrustworthy.

But it's very important to grasp, God is absolutely trustworthy. Just start telling yourself this truth over and over and over, thanking God every single day that He is trustworthy.

*The problem I'm having is there are times when I have nightmares about what happened to me when I was a kid. When she locked me in that room, I was scared and screaming 'til I lost my voice. I wake up in a cold sweat . . . like I've been in a shower.*

Sometimes unresolved issues find expression through nightmares. I want us to cover certain things you can do every time you have a memory of that scene.

*Okay.*

What J. D. needed was hope—hope that he could heal from the pain and horror of this traumatic incident. I knew he would find that hope in God's Word. I suggested we revisit the scene but cast it in a very different light. My prayer was that peace would soon replace panic.

I asked J. D. to picture himself as a little boy standing in that frightening room but to also envision Jesus standing next to him, compassionately whispering gentle assurances. "Do not fear, for I am with you; do not be dismayed, for I am your God. I will strengthen you and help you; I will uphold you with my righteous right hand" (Isa. 41:10).

J. D. needed to understand this was God's message to him *that very day*, to be appropriated back to his terrifying incident when a comforter wasn't present.

I then asked J. D. to picture something else. I wanted him to view himself as a helpless little lamb at the tender age of five, being held in the strong arms of Jesus. And Jesus would again, as He firmly embraced J. D., provide those gentle reassurances of Isaiah 41:10.

When terror would begin to sweep over J. D.'s heart, mind, and spirit, I wanted him to grab hold of that truth. I encouraged him to literally claim Isaiah 41:10 and to say, "Thank You, Lord Jesus, that You hold me and tell me, 'Do not fear, for I am with you.'"

J. D. desperately needed biblical truth—to give him biblical hope that would result in an anchored life. Along the journey he would discover that his heavenly Father is absolutely trustworthy and able to redeem the most revolting situations and bring the kind of healing that can come only from above.

You too can claim the Word of God for your healing. You too can trust His sovereign reign both in and over your life.

## DIVINE DELIVERANCE

The Bible contains many, many stories involving trust in the sovereignty of God amidst the most troubling circumstances. One such story tested a man and an entire nation, and God powerfully proved Himself as the One who alone reigns.

Imagine you were born into slavery, a despised foreigner in a strange land, doomed to a life of backbreaking labor. You have no chance of escape, nowhere to go if you could, and no hope that life will ever be different for you or your descendants.

Then one day a man walks out of the wilderness and tells you God has heard your cries of hopelessness and despair. He delivers this message:

> I am the LORD, and I will bring you out from under the yoke of the Egyptians. I will free you from being slaves to them, and I will redeem you with an outstretched arm and with mighty acts of judgment. I will take you as my own people, and I will be your God. (Ex. 6:6–7)

## TOO GOOD?

That sounds pretty good; maybe *too* good. You'd like to believe it, but this guy Moses, the God-ordained emancipator, was raised in the royal courts of Egypt and was adopted by the pharaoh's daughter. Why would he get involved with sweaty, suffering Hebrew slaves? Could he really be trusted? Could *God* be trusted if Moses was indeed His choice?

What you don't realize is that Moses, actually a fellow Hebrew, has spent the last forty years in the wilderness being prepared by God for your great day of deliverance. When Moses first approaches Pharaoh about letting the Hebrew people go, he is met with contempt and scoffing remarks, culminating in Pharaoh's cruelly increasing the slaves' workload.

The slave nation, millions strong, turns against Moses with disdain and disappointment. And so do you. Did God pick the wrong man for the job, and if so, does that mean God can't be fully trusted? But all doubt begins to dissipate when the Egyptian-cherished Nile River turns into blood.

Through Moses, God begins to intervene in mighty ways, manifesting His awesome sovereignty before the Hebrews and Egyptians alike. You watch in awe as one horrific plague after another afflicts the Egyptians: Water turns to blood; livestock perish; dreadful boils blanket their skin; frogs, gnats, flies, hail, locusts, even darkness cover the now impaired empire.

Finally a mysterious angel of death kills every firstborn child, young and old, rich and poor, as well as the firstborn of all the livestock. But through it all, you and your people are protected and spared.

At last Pharaoh relents and agrees to let you and your people go with Moses into the desert. Rather than hold you back, the Egyptians hastily push you forward, fearing for their very lives if you stay in their country another minute!

Additionally God impresses them to give you whatever you want on your way out, and the former slave nation plunders an empire. *Power . . . protection . . . provision . . .* Now can you trust in the absolute sovereignty of God?

The triumphant procession streams into the wilderness. Everyone is talking about Moses' victory over Pharaoh and the bright future awaiting them. Then the joyfulness gets a jolt when a thunderous rumbling is heard at the rear of the crowd. The sound of pounding hoofbeats and the grinding wheels of chariots grows ever louder, and your greatest fear is realized: *The enemy is not yet defeated.*

The Egyptian army is in hot pursuit, and you and your people face another horrendous hurdle, for stretching before you is a large body of water, the Red Sea. One word flashes across your mind—*trapped*—and again the sovereignty of God is called into question. Panic breaks out. Everyone looks to Moses in bewilderment and outrage. What is going on? Full of desperation and cynicism they inquire:

> Is it because there are no graves in Egypt that you have taken us away to die in the wilderness? What have you done to us in bringing us out of Egypt? (Ex. 14:11 ESV)

God has just delivered the Hebrew people out of one seemingly hopeless situation, but now they doubt that He can deliver them out of a second one. What about you—do you remember God's words delivered through Moses? "I will take you as my own people, and I will be your God" (Ex. 6:7). Does that sound like God's plan involves a burial plot?

Moses responds to the Israelites in complete trust and full of hope, modeling absolute assurance in the promises of God: "Do not be afraid. Stand firm and you will see the deliverance the LORD will bring you today. The Egyptians you see today you will never see again. The LORD will fight for you; you need only to be still" (Ex. 14:13–14).

Again the miraculous occurs. Moses stretches out his hand over the Red Sea, and a strong wind divides the waters, creating a wall on both the right and the left.

The Israelites cross *on dry land*, but God throws the Egyptian army into confusion, and now it's their turn to fear when a realization reverberates throughout their shaken spirits—"Let's get away from the Israelites! The LORD is fighting for them against Egypt" (Ex. 14:25).

It turns out to be too late for a getaway. God instructs Moses to once again stretch his hand out over the sea, and the walls of water come crashing over the Egyptian army, drowning every last soldier. *Delivered once again, in the most daunting of circumstances.*

## THE PRIORITY OF GOD'S PROMISES

And what about us? When storms swell and threaten to overpower us, do we respond like the Israelites, *fearful and hopeless*, or do we respond like Moses, *fearless and hopeful*? The miraculous exodus of the Israelites from Egypt should serve as a constant reminder to have hope in seemingly hopeless situations, because our all-powerful God is *sovereign* over all and totally is trustworthy.

In Romans chapter 4, the apostle Paul recounts the story of God's promise of hope to Abraham—God would make him the father of a great nation, with descendants as numerous as the stars.

There was just one problem with this plan—years had passed, and now at age ninety, Sarah was beyond the ability to bear a baby—and at age one hundred, Abraham was beyond the ability to beget a baby! Neither had the capability to conceive a son. Nevertheless, Scripture states:

> Against all hope, Abraham in hope believed and so became the father of many nations, just as it had been said to him, "So shall your offspring be." Without weakening in his faith, he faced the fact that his body was as good as dead—since he was about a hundred years old—and that Sarah's womb was also dead. Yet he did not waver through unbelief regarding the promise of God, but was strengthened in his faith and gave glory to God, being fully persuaded that God had power to do what he had promised.[5]

When you feel like your hope in God's promises is sinking, remember those wonderful phrases: "Against all hope, Abraham in hope believed . . . he did not waver through unbelief regarding the promise of God . . . fully persuaded that God had power to do what he had promised."

There are times when we, too, must hope against hope.

In such times, remember that we serve the same God who delivered on His promise to Abraham and Sarah and so many others. He still keeps His promises.

On the surface, God's promise seemed beyond belief . . . beyond all hope. Yet even though the fulfillment of this promise looked hopeless . . . "against all hope" . . . Abraham still had hope *in the God of hope.*

The confident hope that Abraham exhibited was not based on *what* was promised but on *who* gave the promise. For indeed what was promised was humanly impossible, but He who gave the promise made it all possible.

The extraordinary reality is this: *The God of the Bible can make the impossible possible.* Luke 1:37 makes this point crystal clear: "Nothing is impossible with God." Therein is your *real hope.* And this hope is factual reality, not fanciful thinking.

## HOPE IS A CHOICE

A Holocaust survivor once inscribed, "I believe in the sun even when it is not shining. I believe in love even when feeling it not. I believe in God even when He is silent."[6]

Like a ship's anchor hidden far beneath the water's surface, God is at work in our lives even when we don't see Him . . . even when we can't hear Him. So when our faith falters, remember, we don't need to see, we don't need to hear, we just need to *trust.* Jesus is our Anchor . . . our sovereign Captain . . . securely holding us and overseeing everything that occurs in our lives.

As the psalmist said, "And now, O Lord, for what do I wait? My hope is in you" (Ps. 39:7 ESV). And as the wisest man ever to live on this earth said, "When the storm has swept by, the wicked are gone, but the righteous stand firm forever" (Prov. 10:25).

# Anchoring Your Hope:
## Keeping an Even Keel

If you ask any mariner, "What is the most important part of a sail-boat?" you might get a variety of answers: "A sound hull for staying afloat." "A mast and a sail for catching the wind." "A rudder for steering the right direction."

But to keep the boat upright during a storm, there is one indispensable part . . . the keel. It is unseen and hidden below the surface of the water, but without it a brisk breeze can blow a large sailboat over on its side or force it to stray off course. When sailing in a strong wind, you need a sturdy keel.

On many boats, the keel resembles an upside-down shark's fin that slices through the water beneath the hull. When a forceful wind on the sail causes the craft to heel, to lean to one side, the keel provides a counterforce that prevents it from flipping over. It also keeps the boat moving forward instead of drifting sideways across the water's surface.

Finally, the keel gives structural strength to the entire boat, holding it together when the swirling action of wind and waves could tear it apart. Traditional boat builders always begin construction with the keel because of its importance to the ship's overall design and integrity.

Storms are inevitable in life. But when the winds begin to blow, your hope in the living God is your "keel" to keep you upright and moving in the right direction. Just like a boat's keel, hope isn't optional but rather is an essential part of the Creator's design for your life.

The following prayer from the Bible reflects a heart of hope based on God's promises: "Sustain me according to your promise, and I will live; do not let my hopes be dashed" (Ps. 119:116).

You may not always feel that hope is at work when blustering waves are battering you on every side. But when your hope is in God, you can know He is holding you together . . . keeping you on course . . . assuring your safety . . . just as He promised.

# 7

# AN ANCHOR LIKE NO OTHER

## HOPE IN THE SAVIOR, JESUS

---

*Jesus: A Star to Steer By*

---

It was *unthinkable* that the ship could be *sinkable*.[1] Sixteen watertight compartments would keep *Titanic* afloat *no matter what!*

Most are familiar with the tragic tale of the *Titanic's* maiden voyage and the nightmare that unfolded in April 1912. The second in a trio of luxury liners, the *Titanic* was designed to glide across the ocean with regal opulence that until then had never been seen.

But just four days after *Titanic* launched from Southampton, England, Captain Smith ignored not one, not two, but *five* ice warnings, deciding not to slow down and proceed with caution but rather to go full steam ahead.

By the time a lookout spotted a formidable iceberg about thirty feet high two hundred yards dead ahead, there was not enough time for the massive ship to steer clear. Colliding with the ship like a razor-sharp diamond, the iceberg slashed a three-hundred-foot-long gash along *Titanic's* starboard hull.

One researcher noted that even with a damaged hull, the ship could have floated until the rescue ship arrived to save all on board. Instead *Titanic* owner J. Bruce Ismay, son of the founder of the White Star Line, a proud and impatient man, perceived the damage to be minimal. Since the ship's pumps appeared to be successfully expelling incoming water, Captain Smith ordered, "Engines ahead, half-speed."[2]

How tragic, because "The inescapable conclusion is that *Titanic's* pumps were swamped by massive amounts of water pushed into the ship by its own forward motion. . . . *Titanic* appears to have steamed itself into a watery North Atlantic grave."[3]

In a matter of minutes the ship's fragile buoyancy gave way, and its fatal plunge began. What was supposed to be unsinkable . . . indestructible . . . split in two at 2:10 A.M. on April 15, 1912. The ship's stern rose out of the ocean, and its massive weight caused the ship to splinter. The bow began a gradual descent into the water while the stern settled atop before it too became submerged.

More than 1,500 of the *Titanic's* estimated 2,200 passengers and crew lost their lives despite the ship's sixteen lifeboats, capable of saving 1,708 people. Owner J. Bruce Ismay did *not* go down with his ship, having boarded one of the lifeboats. Captain Smith, however, was observed standing on the bridge as the icy Atlantic covered the floor beneath him, then finally covered him.

Today countless people live their lives "full steam ahead" as if unaware that at any given moment they, too, could collide with an "iceberg" and find themselves facing an eternity apart from God.

## JUST THE TIP OF THE ICEBERG

On April 14, 1912, the world began to associate a new word with a potentially dreaded danger of traveling by sea: *iceberg*.

The word *iceberg* is borrowed from the Dutch word *ijsberg*, which literally means "ice mountain." An iceberg forms when a large chunk of ice "calves" off, breaking off from the edge of a land-based glacier and falling into the ocean. Ranging from five feet to 650 feet across, icebergs can tower above the icy water to heights of 250 feet or more and can weigh as much as two hundred thousand tons.

But the visible portion of an iceberg doesn't pose the greatest threat to ships. As mountainous as one may appear to cautious mariners, only 10 percent of an iceberg's total size can be seen. Not only does nine-tenths of a floating iceberg stay hidden beneath the waves, but its underwater shape is also impossible to predict due to differences in density between glacial ice and seawater. Therefore, steering a ship close to an iceberg is much too risky.

That's why the phrase, "It's just the tip of the iceberg" is a warning that something is deceptively dangerous. In other words: *Beware—there is far more here than meets the eye!*

When traveling the treacherous waters on your own journey, how can you be sure that the problems you see on the horizon aren't actually ten times larger? You need more than a little human help—you really need God-sized help.

How can you be certain where the real dangers lie? How can you make sure you steer clear without needlessly traveling too far away? The answer is: *You can't.* There will always be unseen perils in your path. No amount of wishful thinking or blind self-reliance will ever change that.

Your hope needs to be placed in the One who sees all . . . the One who knows all. Notice how the Bible describes this One: "Nothing in all creation is hidden from God's sight. Everything is uncovered and laid bare before the eyes of him to whom we must give account."[4]

Seek Him . . . ask Him and trust Him to reveal the "icebergs" in your path that could be catastrophic, that could tear your heart open and capsize your life. Put your hope in Him.

> The LORD is good to those whose hope is in him, to the one who seeks him. (Lam. 3:25)

## THE TRUE HOPE OF *TITANIC*'S LAST HERO[5]

Among the passengers on that first and final voyage of *Titanic* was forty-year-old John Harper, an English pastor, traveling to speak at Chicago's Moody Church.

After the ship struck the iceberg and began to sink, *Titanic* owner J. Bruce Ismay helped others into the lifeboats; then he, too, boarded one. By contrast, Harper secured his six-year-old daughter, Nana, in a lifeboat but apparently made no effort to follow. Instead he called through the crowded deck, "Women, children, and unsaved into the lifeboats!"

Survivors report that Harper began witnessing to anyone within hearing. He continued sharing Christ even after he had jumped into the icy water while clinging to a piece of wreckage, having already given his lifejacket to another man.

Harper's final moments were recounted four years later:

> I am a survivor of the *Titanic*. When I was drifting alone on a spar that awful night, the tide brought Mr. Harper, also on a piece of wreck, near me.
>
> "Man," he said, "are you saved?"
>
> "No," I said, "I am not."
>
> He replied, "Believe on the Lord Jesus Christ and thou shalt be saved."
>
> The waves bore him away, but, strange to say, brought him back a little later, and he said, "Are you saved now?"
>
> "No," I said, "I cannot honestly say that I am."
>
> He said again, "Believe on the Lord Jesus Christ, and thou shalt be saved," and shortly after, he went down; and there, alone in the night, and with two miles of water under me, I believed. I am John Harper's last convert.[6]

This man was one of only six people picked out of the water by the lifeboats; the other 1,517, including Harper, were left to die. Harper staked his life on this biblical truth stated by Jesus Himself:

> Whoever would save his life will lose it, but whoever loses his life for my sake and the gospel's will save it. (Mark 8:35 ESV)

## THE FAILURE OF FALSE HOPE

Unlike Harper, many on the *Titanic* placed their trust in false hope . . . in *Titanic*'s supposed safety . . . in the belief that more lifeboats were unnecessary . . . in the overblown reassurances of the ship's company. More than likely, many of the wealthy on the maiden voyage had a false sense of security in their own invincibility.

But all that false hope was just that—false—and the ship went down. By contrast, John Harper knew where true hope was found. He, too, undoubtedly considered the ship seaworthy and safe. But that night his actions showed that he placed his eternal trust not in the maker of the ship but in the Maker of the seas.

Harper's focus while in the dark freezing ocean was not on this temporal life but on eternal life. His destination was certain, his trust assured, and he wanted others to share that peace-filled promise of eternal life. Until his dying breath, Harper offered the message of hope to all within the sound of his voice.

Many have asked, Why would Harper sacrifice his life for someone considered "unsaved"? How could he have such absolute assurance in Christ? Couldn't he have had misplaced hope? To answer these questions, we will consider the events that occurred after the crucifixion of Christ, the One in whom John Harper trusted so completely.

## LOST AND FOUND: THE RESURRECTION OF TRUE HOPE

Many had confirmed the faith-shattering fact: Jesus was dead. The faithful few had personally seen His arrest, crucifixion, and burial . . . had seen soldiers pierce His body with a spear . . . had seen Him lowered from the cross and taken away. They witnessed His body being wrapped in burial cloths and sealed in a tomb.

Believers all across the city huddled together in shock . . . in sorrow . . . with a mixture of confusion and disillusion.

Three days later, two of His grief-stricken followers were walking to a nearby village. The dusty road on that seven-mile stretch must have seemed much longer that day. Their hearts were heavy with sorrow and full of uncertainty now that Jesus was gone . . . and with Him all of their hopes.

As the two men walked, how could they reconcile the claims of Jesus with His catastrophic death? A gut-wrenching question (How could God die?) haunted them.

A fellow traveler joined them, asking, "What are you discussing?"

One answered, "Are you only a visitor to Jerusalem and do not know the things that have happened there in recent days?"

"What things?" he asked.

They poured out the heart rending story.

About Jesus of Nazareth . . . He was a prophet, powerful in word and deed before God and all the people. The chief priests and our rulers handed him over to be sentenced to death, and they crucified him; but we had hoped that he was the one who was going to redeem Israel. And what is more, it is the third day since all this took place.[7]

The not-so-subtle implication? "We had *hoped* . . . but now He's dead, and our hopes died with Him."

But there's a strange twist to this story, the pair tells the traveler—some women went to His tomb, only to find the stone rolled back and Jesus' body missing! They said angels told them Jesus was *alive*.

The men continued, "Some of those who were with us went to the tomb and found it just as the women had said, but him they did not see."[8]

## BEYOND HUMAN VISION—SPIRITUAL SIGHT

The confusion was unsettling: Was Jesus dead? Was Jesus alive? "If only we could *see* Him."

The hope of these troubled travelers was limited to what they could see. And what had they seen? They saw Him die! They did not see Him alive again, despite the women's accounts to the contrary. Based on the "evidence," how could they believe anything but the worst? How could they ignore the facts? How could they continue to have hope?

Living in our material world conditions us to rely on our five senses as a filter for truth. We commonly reject what we cannot weigh, measure, and describe. Yet the inseparable companion of Christian hope is *faith*, which doesn't operate by sight or sound or any other properties detectable by our physical senses.

Holocaust survivor Corrie ten Boom put it this way: "Faith is like radar that sees through the fog, the reality of things at a distance that the human eye cannot see."[9] At times, however, our "radar" doesn't work . . . our faith begins to falter. It happens to all of us, just as it happened to the disciples. Sometimes the night seems too dark, the fog too dense, and the despair feels too deep.

These two distraught disciples experienced such a moment. But can you imagine what those men must have experienced that day when they heard what they were told by their fellow traveler, who actually was *the resurrected Jesus*?

In essence He said, "Why are you so slow to believe all the prophecies about me?"

"How foolish you are, and how slow of heart to believe all that the prophets have spoken! Did not the Christ have to suffer these things and then enter his glory?" And beginning with Moses and all the Prophets, he explained to them what was said in all the Scriptures concerning himself.[10]

Make no mistake, the central figure in all of Scripture is *Jesus*. The awe-inspiring story of human redemption has been likened to a scarlet thread woven throughout the Bible from Genesis to Revelation. And even before the foundation of the world, it had been determined that Jesus would be the Savior of the world.

No one can refute that a man named Jesus was born in Bethlehem . . . grew up in Nazareth . . . was crucified and buried in Jerusalem. Both Jewish and Roman historians verify the authenticity of His existence as well as His identification as a prophet and a teacher. When it comes to controversy surrounding Jesus Christ, it's not His humanity that's called into question, *it's His claims to deity.*

Jesus repeatedly identified Himself as the Jews' long-awaited Messiah . . . the Christ . . . the very Son of God. But words . . . and an empty tomb . . . have been insufficient evidence for skeptics down through the centuries. Even incredible miracles recorded in the historically reliable Bible don't seem to impress determined doubters.

But one area of study should make *every* skeptic stand at attention. A great body of evidence exists, fully supporting Jesus' claims to be the Messiah (which means "the Anointed One"), sent by God the Father to redeem the world from sin.

Contained within the pages of the Bible are hundreds of messianic prophecies . . . information foretold centuries before the Messiah's birth . . . all pointing directly and *only* to Jesus.

What's more, every single messianic prophecy has been fulfilled, which means the evidence is indisputable that Jesus is precisely who He says He is.

## WHAT ARE THE ODDS?

"Are you aware of the astronomical odds of one man fulfilling all of these hundreds of prophecies? What are the odds . . . mathematically

. . . of someone fulfilling just eight messianic prophecies?" This was a question mathematician Peter Stoner explored with his students at Pasadena City College.[11] Here's what they discovered:

1. *The Messiah would come from the tiny town of Bethlehem* (see Matt. 2:1). Over seven hundred years *before* Jesus was born in Bethlehem, the prophet Micah predicted, "You, Bethlehem Ephrathah, though you are small among the clans of Judah, out of you will come for me one who will be ruler over Israel, whose origins are from old, from ancient times" (Mic. 5:2).

How many men could have possibly fulfilled this prophecy by having been born in Bethlehem? What are the odds of *any one man* being born in Bethlehem? To answer this question, divide the average number of residents of Bethlehem by the average population of the earth from the time of Micah to today.

The earth's population has averaged under two billion people, while Bethlehem's population has averaged about 7,150. Therefore, statistically speaking (in round figures), 1 man in 7,150 divided by 2,000,000,000 (or 1 man in $2.8 \times 10^5$) could have fulfilled this prophecy. So, for *a particular man* to have been born in Bethlehem, the odds are 1 in 280,000.

2. *The Messiah would have a forerunner* (see Matt. 3:11). Over four hundred years *before* Jesus was born, the prophet Malachi predicted (giving the Lord's words), "See, I will send my messenger, who will prepare the way before me" (Mal. 3:1).

The question then becomes, of all the men born in Bethlehem, how many have had a forerunner as described in this prophecy with a specific mission and message from God? What are the odds of *any man* from Bethlehem with a forerunner? Let's employ an *extremely conservative* estimate: The odds are 1 in 1,000. (The total for these two prophecies now stands at $2.8 \times 10^8 = 1$ man in 280,000,000.)

3. *The Messiah would enter Jerusalem as a king riding on a donkey* (see John 12:15). Around five hundred years *before* Jesus was born, the prophet Zechariah predicted, "See, your king comes to you, righteous and having salvation, gentle and riding on a donkey, on a colt, the foal of a donkey" (Zech. 9:9).

Now consider: Of all the people who have ever lived, (1) how many were born in Bethlehem, (2) were preceded by a dynamic messenger from God, and (3) entered Jerusalem as a ruler riding on a donkey? Or let's simply ask, "How many kings—*born anywhere*—have ridden into Jerusalem on a donkey?"

What are the odds? To be extremely, *extremely conservative*, let's say the odds are 1 in 100. (The total for all three prophecies now stands at $2.8 \times 10^{10} = 1$ man in 28,000,000,000.)

4. *The Messiah would be betrayed by a friend and wounded as a result* (see Luke 22:47–48). "One shall say unto him, What are these wounds in thine hands? Then he shall answer, Those with which I was wounded in the house of my friends" (Zech. 13:6 KJV).

This prediction raises the question, "One man in how many from Bethlehem rode into Jerusalem on a donkey and was then betrayed by a friend, with the result that his hands were wounded"? What are the odds?

Though most betrayals by close friends don't result in physical wounds, an *extremely conservative* estimate would be: The odds are 1 in 1,000. (The total for the four prophecies now stands at $2.8 \times 10^{13} = 1$ man in 28,000,000,000,000.)

5. *The Messiah would be betrayed for exactly thirty pieces of silver* (see Matt. 26:15). "They paid me thirty pieces of silver" (Zech. 11:12).

What are the odds that this messianic prophecy could name *the precise amount* . . . especially when it could have been *any amount*? For the Messiah's betrayer to be paid *exactly* thirty pieces of silver . . . not gold or anything else . . . let's say, being *extremely conservative*, the odds are 1 in 1,000. (The total for the five prophecies now stands at $2.8 \times 10^{16}$ = 1 man in 28,000,000,000,000,000.)

6. *The Messiah's betrayer would throw down his blood money in the temple, and it would become the potter's possession* (see Matt. 27:3, 10). "The LORD said to me, 'Throw it to the potter'—the handsome price at which they priced me! So I took the thirty pieces of silver and threw them into the house of the LORD to the potter" (Zech. 11:13).

What are the odds that one man in how many would be betrayed for thirty pieces of silver that were thrown down in the temple and eventually became the possession of the potter? To be *extremely conservative*, the odds are 1 in 100,000. (The total for all six prophecies now stands at $2.8 \times 10^{21} = 1$ man in 2,800,000,000,000,000,000,000.)

7. *The Messiah would be an innocent, beaten man whose life is on the line, yet he would remain silent when offered a chance to defend himself* (see Matt. 26:63, 67–68). Interestingly, seven hundred years *before* Jesus was born, the prophet Isaiah presented an amazing profile of the Messiah, including this prediction: "He was oppressed and afflicted, yet he did not open his mouth; he was led like a lamb to the slaughter, and as a sheep before her shearers is silent, so he did not open his mouth. . . . He was assigned a grave with the wicked, and with the rich in his death, though he had done no violence, nor was any deceit in his mouth" (Isa. 53:7, 9).

What are the odds that an innocent man who is oppressed, afflicted, and on trial for his life would not open his mouth to defend himself in spite of his innocence? To calculate the likelihood for this very unlikely chain of events, let's make an *extremely conservative* estimate: The odds are 1 in 1,000. (The total for these seven prophecies now stands at $2.8 \times 10^{24} = 1$ man in 2,800,000,000,000,000,000,000,000.)

8. *The Messiah would be crucified* (see Luke 23:23). Imagine that ten centuries before the birth of Jesus, a messianic psalm was written predicting the manner of death that the Messiah would experience, specifically detailing the anguish of crucifixion, although that form of death had not yet been devised. Psalm 22:14–16 reads, "I am poured out like water, and all my bones are out of joint . . . a band of evil men has encircled me, they have pierced my hands and my feet."

Realizing that crucifixion was a later invention (around the fifth century B.C.) and that only a very small percentage of the population was actually crucified, what are the odds that any man would have died of crucifixion? To be *extremely conservative*, the odds are 1 in 10,000. (The total of all eight of the prophecies finally stands at $2.8 \times 10^{28} = 1$ man in 28,000,000,000,000,000,000,000,000,000.)

Ultimately, Peter Stoner calculated the likelihood of *any one man* living from the time these eight predictions were made down to the present day and fulfilling all eight predictions to be 1 in $10^{17}$ or *one chance in a hundred million billion*.

He likens the odds to placing a hundred million billion silver dollars across the state of Texas, a quantity that would be enough to cover it two feet deep from north to south and east to west. Then suppose a blindfolded man reaching down into the sea of silver dollars would, on his first attempt, pick up one . . . *the only one* . . . that had been specially marked. Those are the odds!

9. *And what are the odds of the virgin birth* . . . Isaiah's prediction that the Messiah would be born of a virgin, without the seed of a man (Isa. 7:14; see Luke 1:26–35)? The odds are unimaginable.

10. *Likewise, what are the odds of the Resurrection* . . . the fulfillment of David's prediction that the Messiah would rise from the dead, never to experience death again (Ps. 16:10; see Luke chapter 24)? The odds are incalculable.

The only person who has fulfilled all these prophecies and thus revealed *the true identity* of the promised Messiah is Jesus of Nazareth. As John the Baptist declared when he first saw Jesus, "Behold, the Lamb of God, who takes away the sin of the world!" (John 1:29 ESV).

## HOPE YOU CAN COUNT ON

Now do you see why Christian hope is anything but some pie-in-the-sky, ethereal concept? It is a rock-solid *guaranteed assurance* that Jesus is who He claims to be, God Himself, the Second Person of the Trinity. What He promises for us will come true.

Now do you understand why you can have hope in Jesus . . . why He is the one and only Anchor you will ever need? Jesus is God . . . therefore Jesus is sovereign over all storms, all circumstances in your life. He is indeed the resurrected Lord.

Amidst the prophetic truths verifying Jesus as Messiah, one day we'll see the very same physical "proofs" that Jesus presented to His disciples as confirmation that He indeed was the one who hung on that cross, died, and was resurrected. "Why are you troubled, and why do doubts rise in your minds? Look at my hands and my feet. It is I myself! Touch me and see; a ghost does not have flesh and bones, as you see I have" (Luke 24:38–39).

Jesus' nail-scarred hands and feet will forever remind us in heaven that we are only there because of *Him*, because of His substitutionary death in our place—mine and *yours*.

## THE LIFESAVER RESCUE PLAN

Jesus endured a magnitude 5 "spiritual hurricane." But why did that happen? It has everything to do with the word *saved*.

Just *how* has Jesus saved us? More than two thousand years ago, He died on a cross for our sins, taking our punishment and rescuing us from an eternity separated from Him. Jesus rose from the dead and today offers the gift of eternal life to all who place their trust in Him.

And He offers us something more . . . the gift of biblical hope . . . so that we, like John Harper, can know with 100 percent assurance where we're going when we die.

What does the person drowning in the water need? The desperate need is to be saved. That person going under needs a savior, a rescuer, which is why God in His infinite mercy and grace offers us a *Lifesaver Rescue Plan*. Here's how it works:

When God created the universe, He gave all human beings free will . . . the freedom to go *against* His will (this is called sin).

From the beginning of human history, God made His will clearly known, but the first two people He created chose to go against His will.

God knows that we all have sinned. The problem is this: The Bible says our sins *separate us* from God. But God doesn't want us separated from Him—He wants to save us.

And that's the "why" of Jesus. Jesus, who is God, left heaven and came to earth. Although He lived a perfect life, He was crucified on a cross. He wasn't a victim—His life was not taken from Him—He gave His life as a ransom for many. He chose to take the punishment for our sins upon Himself—to become our heavenly Lifesaver. In His death, He chose to take our sin so that if we would receive Him as our personal Lord and Savior, He would forgive us of *all* of our sin. That means sin no longer separates us from God.

The Bible says that those who trust Jesus to anchor their lives not only gain eternal salvation but also a guaranteed hope and help, purpose and peace. And God promises a life-changing relationship with Him now and the ultimate gift of eternal life in heaven. God has made the way; He has cleared the decks to secure your salvation.

Respecting your will, He won't force His way into your heart though. Instead He is gently inviting you to accept Jesus as your Lord and Savior. When you surrender the helm, the control of your life to Him, He will save you and give you hope that lasts forever . . . a hope found only in an anchored life relationship with Him.

Every competent captain spends hours studying the maps, then charting the course in order to reach the desired destination.

And God gave us His chart . . . a way for all of us to sail safely across the mysterious and sometimes perilous "oceans" of life. As we place our faith in Him to lead, guide, and protect us, He promises to keep us from drifting hopelessly off course in our lives.

It works the same way when it comes to hope. We have a guaranteed hope given to us by God. He promises to guide us into all wisdom and onto the right path. Proverbs 4:11 (esv) says, "I have taught you the way of wisdom; I have led you in the paths of uprightness."

## THE PLAN WITH FOUR PARTS
The Lord Himself is your hope. . . . He is your guide. . . . He is "the way and the truth and the life" (John 14:6).

Follow this four-point plan to chart your course with Christ, your Lifesaver:

### 1. God's Purpose for You . . . Is *Salvation*
God sent Christ to earth to express His love for you by saving you. The Bible says:

> God so loved the world that he gave his one and only Son, that who-ever believes in him shall not perish but have eternal life. For God did not send his Son into the world to condemn the world, but to save the world through him.[12]

Jesus came to earth to forgive your sins, empower you to have victory over sin, and enable you to live a fulfilled life, anchored in Him! Jesus said, "I have come that they may have life, and have it to the full."[13]

## 2. Your Problem . . . Is *Sin*

Sin is living independently of God's standard—knowing what is right, but choosing what is wrong. The Bible says, "Anyone, then, who knows the good he ought to do and doesn't do it, sins."[14]

The consequence of sin is spiritual death . . . eternal separation from God. Because God is just, this penalty must be paid by someone— either you or a substitute. Scripture states:

> Your iniquities [sins] have separated you from your God. . . . For the wages of sin is death, but the gift of God is eternal life in Christ Jesus our Lord.[15]

## 3. God's Provision for You . . . Is the *Savior*

Jesus died on the cross to personally pay the penalty for your sins.

> God demonstrates his own love for us in this: While we were still sinners, Christ died for us.[16]

Belief in (entrusting your life to) Jesus Christ to be your Lifesaver, who paid the penalty for your sins, is the *only way* to have a personal relationship with God the Father. Jesus says:

> I am the way and the truth and the life. No one comes to the Father except through me.[17]

## 4. Your Part . . . Is *Surrender*

Give Christ control of your life—entrusting yourself to Him.

> Jesus said to his disciples, "If anyone would come after me, he must deny himself and take up his cross [die to your own self-rule] and follow me. For whoever wants to save his life will lose it, but whoever loses his life for me will find it. What good will it be for a man if he gains the whole world, yet forfeits his soul?"[18]

Place your faith in (rely on) Jesus Christ as your personal Lord and Savior and reject your good works—or any other method—as a way to earn God's approval.

It is by grace you have been saved, through faith—and this not from yourselves, it is the gift of God—not by works, so that no one can boast.[19]

Hope starts here! The moment you choose to receive Jesus as your Lord and Savior—entrusting your life to Him—He comes to live inside you. Then He gives you His power to live the fulfilled life God has planned for you. If you want to be fully forgiven by God, receive the gift of eternal life, and become the person God created you to be, you can tell Him in a simple, heartfelt prayer, perhaps one similar to the one I prayed many years ago:

> God, I need hope—hope for my life.
>> Most of all, I need You in my life.
>> I admit I've sinned. Please forgive me.
>> Thank You, Jesus, for dying on the cross for my sins.
>> Come into my life as my Lord and Savior and make me the kind of
> person you want me to be. In Your strong name I pray. Amen.

## WHAT CAN YOU EXPECT NOW?

If you sincerely prayed this prayer, here is what God says to you:

> They who wait for the LORD shall renew their strength; they shall mount up with wings like eagles; they shall run and not be weary; they shall walk and not faint. (Isa. 40:31 ESV)

Life with Christ is endless hope. Without Him it's a hopeless end. You cannot know *what* the future holds, but you can know *who* holds the future—your glorious Lifesaver. And that, my friend, is all you need to know!

## Anchoring Your Hope:
## A Star to Steer By

On land, giving directions is not really difficult. It is a matter of splitting the journey up—no matter how long—into smaller segments. The trick is to move from landmark to landmark, eventually arriving at your destination. *Head away from town, passing by that abandoned blue hotel. At the first stop sign, turn right, then go about a mile until you see the red hay barn. Turn right again on the dirt road, and that will take you straight to the Hamburger Hut by the lake!*

But how would you give directions if there were no landmarks to signal the need to turn one way or another? Or for that matter, what if there were no roads? What if the landscape itself never looked any different . . . except for the time of day or the weather?

Now imagine being one of the earliest sailors with precisely this dilemma. How could you navigate across vast expanses of ocean with no visible landmarks? The slightest error in judgment could mean arriving hundreds of miles from your intended destination. And one single storm could cause your expedition to be hopelessly lost.

Your problem is solved, however, because astronomers have discovered you no longer need to look at the horizon for help—instead, look up . . . at the sky. *Celestial navigation* makes use of the sun, moon, planets, or one of fifty-seven navigational stars whose positions and movements are easy to calculate and pinpoint throughout the year. Despite how it appears to the untrained observer, all celestial bodies in the sky move in precise, exact, predictable ways.

Using a device called a sextant, you (and other ancient mariners) can measure the angle between a star in the sky and the horizon. By using this information, you can identify your ship's exact position on the globe! The whole process was made possible by the absolute, unchanging reliability of the stars and planets.

Today that function is performed by GPS (Global Positioning System) satellites that triangulate a ship's location from space by the touch of a button. (Triangulation is a measurement technique that uses a network of triangles to divide the earth's surface in order to locate one specific position on the earth.)

Yet for all of this impressive technological precision, such machines cannot compete with the stars for unerring infallibility and dependability. Satellites are vulnerable to all sorts of disruptions—from catastrophic collisions with space debris to hardware malfunctions and software glitches. As is so often the case in our technological world, expediency and convenience have replaced consistency.

Too frequently we experience unexpected glitches in our personal lives as well. To navigate the sometimes difficult waters of everyday life, you can make the mistake of "looking at the horizon" as far as your eyes can see—and yet still get off course. Beware of placing all your hope in human solutions that inevitably fail or fall short.

Anything made by human beings can eventually wear out, run down, or fall apart. But God always has been and always will be unchangeable, unalterable, and unshakable. The Bible says He is "the same yesterday and today and forever."[20]

The first and foremost person to look to for guidance is Jesus Himself. By following His example, we will become increasingly wise and discerning. Jesus said, "I am the light of the world. Whoever follows me will not walk in darkness, but will have the light of life" (John 8:12 ESV).

Consider this course of action: Since the Bible calls Jesus "the bright morning star,"[21] look even higher than the celestial bodies and put your hope in the Supreme Star, who promises to guide you and direct you. He will never fail to show you the way home.

# 8

# THE RIGHT MAP WILL
# LIGHT YOUR WAY

## HOPE IN THE WORD OF GOD

*God's Word:*
*A Map to Navigate By*

---

If you ever want to experience just how pitch-black total darkness can be, take a tour of Carlsbad Caverns in New Mexico.

At first you follow a smooth, well-lit pathway that winds downward into the cool, damp earth. You see beautiful and unusual formations of stone shaped through time by the slow growth of minerals dissolved in groundwater. As you move deeper into the cavern, stillness and silence increasingly close in around you.

At some point your tour guide stops to tell you about the cave's discoverers. They faced formidable obstacles as they explored the dangerous terrain now so easy for you to walk on . . . now covered by pavement. And what was their biggest challenge? *Darkness.*

To show visitors what it was like for those brave souls, suddenly the cavern lights go out. Startled exclamations and nervous laughter erupt from surprised tourists. Then a sense of uneasiness surges through you. You want to find some sort of railing to hold on to, but you can't see a thing.

As the lights remain off for what seems like a long time, you begin to think, *What if they don't come back on? I can't see where to step. What if I can't find my way out?* The darkness is so dense, you can't see your hand in front of your face. The novelty of the cavern quickly fades. Without proper supervision, Carlsbad Caverns could be a tourist attraction turned terrifying.

Now imagine for a moment you are there alone in your subterranean world. Mounting apprehension gives way to full-fledged anxiety and finally to heart-pounding fear. *Should I walk along the cave walls and "feel" my way out? What if there's a dangerous drop-off? How far could I possibly fall?* At this point, what would you give for a flashlight or a candle or a match . . . anything that could shed a little light?

Sometimes people who have fallen into the darkest pit of despair call in during *Hope In The Night.* Thinking there is no way out, their emotions run the gamut. They are often angry and afraid, guilty and grieving, lonely and lost. They call, begging for someone to give them the light of hope.

As the program begins each night, I feel humbled because I know the Lord will lead certain callers to call and certain hearers to hear God's truth that can set them free. *Hope* is what they seek, and *hope* is what they find when they grasp God's truth . . . the light we all need. The key verse for *Hope In The Night* actually focuses on moving from darkness to light: "You are my lamp, O Lord; the Lord turns my darkness into light" (2 Sam. 22:29).

Light chases the darkness out of every corner . . . from every nook and cranny of our lives. Light has the power to transform everything on which it shines. Jesus said, "I am the light of the world."[1]

And He invites you and me to become *reflectors* of His light. "You are the light of the world . . . let your light shine before men, that they may see your good deeds and praise your Father in heaven" (Matt. 5:14–16).

## THE LAMP THAT NEVER BURNS OUT

If you feel like you're living life in Carlsbad Caverns . . . directionless, desperate, despairing . . . God has a lamp He'd like to place in your hands. It will faithfully guide you every day of your life, and its light can never be snuffed out. That lamp is the tried and true Word of God. The psalmist understood this when he wrote, "Your word is a lamp to my feet and a light to my path."[2] Indeed, God's Word illumines the darkest cave, sheds light in the murkiest of tunnels, and, most importantly, shows us the way out.

How well I remember a time when I knew nothing about the Word of God. Oh, I had a Bible, but I never opened it. I attended a church, but no one brought a Bible with them. There was no Bible *study* and no real appreciation for the rich truths that would make such an undertaking worthwhile.

Eventually the Lord put me in a biblically based church, and what an experience! We were continually turning the pages of Scripture, though initially those sitting next to me had to help me find the right references. As one Bible teacher amusingly commented, "June is just like a blank page." How true it was!

Never before had I heard the Bible taught with such power. Soon I began to live for Sundays. I was so excited that I could hear God's basic plan and purpose for life . . . even *my* life. I was learning directly from the Bible about creation, history, and "His story."

But, although I liked what I was learning, how could I have a rational, reasonable assurance that the Bible itself was true? I was a logical thinker . . . I loved math . . . and therefore I did not want to be swayed emotionally or to place my hope in something half true.

While I was being exposed to biblical truth on Sundays, my high school history teacher was giving multiple reasons to disbelieve the Scriptures during the week. He attempted to discredit the Bible with certain arguments.

*Argument #1* involved "the Exodus" in Exodus chapter 14. He said no miracle occurred when Moses led the two million Israelites out of Egyptian bondage. They did not cross through the middle of the Red Sea on dry ground; rather they crossed the Sea of Reeds, which was only a few inches deep. There was no miraculous parting of the deep waters.

After hearing this explanation, I told my Bible teacher, "I understand that Moses didn't really perform a miracle by parting the Red Sea . . . it was only the shallow Reed Sea." Without hesitation my wise teacher exclaimed, "Why, that's an even greater miracle! The entire Egyptian army, in hot pursuit of the Israelites, drowned in only a few inches of water!" I smiled . . . and kept smiling.

*Argument #2* concerned supposed "conflicting biblical accounts." My history teacher stated that the Bible contains obvious contradictions. The Gospel of Matthew presents Jesus miraculously feeding the *five* thousand, whereas Mark's Gospel presents Jesus feeding *four* thousand.

However, when I later read both Matthew and Mark, to my surprise I discovered that *both* Gospels detail *two different accounts* of Jesus miraculously feeding four thousand and miraculously feeding five thousand people. (See for yourself in Matthew chapters 14 and 15, also in Mark chapters 6 and 8.) Why is it presumed that there was only *one* miraculous mega-feast? Obviously there is no contradiction.

Early in my search for truth I heard people say, "The Bible is basically a book of history, poetry, and *mythology*. How can any intelligent person put hope in such an unreliable book?"

The first major defense I heard for the reliability and validity of Scripture was in the realm of prophecy. Of all the world's designated "holy books," the Bible alone contains prophecies, with one exception. In Islam, there is one *self-fulfilling* prophecy in the Qu'ran that refers to Muhammad.

In contrast, the Bible contains many prophecies that have been fulfilled and recorded in history . . . not just in the Bible. The astronomical odds for the fulfillment of so many prophecies alone validates the truthfulness and reliability of the Bible.

Two points are helpful to understand. First, the apostle Peter explains, "No prophecy of Scripture came about by the prophet's own interpretation. For prophecy never had its origin in the will of man, but men spoke from God as they were carried along by the Holy Spirit" (2 Pet. 1:20–21). In other words, these supernatural occurrences have a supernatural source . . . God Himself.

And secondly, many people don't realize the scientific truths contained within the pages of Scripture. I continue to be absolutely amazed at this area of study and the support it gives to the truthfulness and reliability of the Bible.

For those who ask, "Can I really place my *hope* in the promises of the Bible?" I answer, "Absolutely!" Let me explain.

## SCIENTIFIC TRUTHS IN THE BIBLE[3]

Even though the Bible is not a science textbook, it reveals many scientific facts . . . and the Bible never contradicts true science. In truth, the Bible bore witness to the following facts . . . *long before scientists ever "discovered" them too.*

### 1. Geophysics: The Earth Is Round, a Circular Sphere[4]

For thousands of years, most people believed the earth was flat. Until the sixteenth century when astronomers Copernicus and Kepler postulated otherwise, only a few philosophers opposed the prevalent belief that a ship could sail off the edge of the earth!

This scientific theory held fast until the invention of the compass and Magellan's voyage in 1521. Being the first person to circle the globe, Magellan demonstrated that a ship could continually travel west or east around the world and return to its original point of departure without falling off the earth!

However, this scientific truth had been revealed in the Bible more than 2,300 years before Magellan by the prophet Isaiah in the eighth century B.C. Obviously Isaiah did not get his wisdom from the science of his day, which taught that the earth was flat, for he proclaimed, "He [God] sits enthroned above the *circle* of the earth" (Isa. 40:22). The Hebrew word *chug* means "circle, sphere, circuit."[5] The earth Isaiah described was indeed a circular sphere.

### 2. Planetology: The Earth Is Suspended in Space[6]

During the time when the book of Job was written, the most advanced scientific theory presented planet earth as flat. Earth was believed to be carried on the back of a gigantic turtle swimming through some cosmic sea.

Later theories presented the earth as carried on the back of a tiger or an elephant. (The shaking of the elephant accounted for earthquakes.) Only in the seventeenth century A.D. did the scientific community, with the help of Newton's gravitational theory, discover the force that propels celestial bodies through space.

However, this scientific truth had been revealed in the Bible much earlier in the book of Job, written around the fifteenth century B.C.: "He [God] spreads out the northern skies over empty space; he suspends the earth over nothing" (Job 26:7).

### 3. Astronomy: The Stars Cannot Be Counted[7]

For thousands of years during Old Testament times, the number of stars in the skies was considered to be between twelve hundred and four thousand as seen by the naked eye. In A.D. 150 the world-renowned astronomer Ptolemy emphatically stated the exact number of stars to be 1,056.

Yet earlier, around 2000 B.C., God had told Abraham, "'Look up at the heavens and count the stars—if indeed you can count them.' Then he said to him, 'So shall your offspring be'" (Gen. 15:5). Within a short time Abraham had more than four thousand descendants, later numbering in the millions. Was the Bible wrong? No.

With the scientific invention of the telescope in 1609, followed by the Hubble telescope in the 1990s, scientists today declare the stars to be as numerous as the sands of the sea. Astronomers estimate that there are at least 10 to the $26^{th}$ power—that is a hundred million billion billion stars. If you could count ten numbers per second, it would take you at least a thousand million billion years to count to that number.[8]

However, this scientific truth had been revealed in the Bible from God to Abraham some 3,700 years before the telescope was invented: "I will surely bless you and make your descendants as numerous as the stars in the sky and as the sand on the seashore" (Gen. 22:17).

### 4. Earth Science: Mountains and Canyons Exist in the Sea[9]

For thousands of years, until the twentieth century, the scientific assumption was that the ocean was bowl-shaped—shallow around the edges and deepest in the middle. Yet today researchers have discovered that some of the highest mountains and deepest valleys exist in the middle of oceans, including the Atlantic range. In the Pacific Ocean, the Mariana Trench near the Philippines is over seven miles deep.

However, this scientific truth had been revealed in the Bible several thousand years earlier. In the tenth century B.C., David spoke of "the valleys of the sea" (2 Sam. 22:16). In the eighth century B.C., rebellious Jonah described sinking to the bottom of a submerged mountain after being thrown overboard: "To the *roots of the mountains* I sank down" (Jonah 2:6).

## 5. Oceanography: Springs and Fountains Exist in the Sea

For thousands of years, people were unaware of the hidden springs and fountains on the sea floor. Then, after World War II, research ships discovered underwater volcanoes, and today more than ten thousand have been cataloged. Researcher Dr. William Rubey of the U.S. Geological Survey reports that each year 430 tons of water are released from underwater volcanic outlets.[10] The heat from the volcanic activity forces the entrapped water out through one of these natural openings.

However, this scientific truth had been revealed much earlier in several books of the Bible. In the fifteenth century B.C., the first book of the Bible described Noah as having entered the ark when "*All the springs* of the great deep burst forth, and the floodgates of the heavens were opened." Then, after forty days and nights, "The *springs of the deep* and the floodgates of the heavens had been closed" (Gen. 7:11; 8:2). In the tenth century B.C., the Bible says of the Creator God, "He established the clouds above and fixed securely the *fountains of the deep*" (Prov. 8:28).

## 6. Hematology: Life Is in the Blood[11]

Bloodletting was a widespread, medical procedure practiced among many peoples for some three thousand years, until the early twentieth century. The medical community believed that any disease could be treated by removing a sizable amount of blood from a patient. Scientists and surgeons believed that bloodletting would remove stagnant blood building up in the extremities.

The more severe the problem, the more blood would be "let," whether by lances or leeches. But the truth is, bloodletting caused many illnesses to escalate in severity, even to the point of death. Suffering with a throat infection in 1799, George Washington, the first president of the

United States, had approximately four pints (1.7 liters) of blood removed from his body, a process that contributed to his death.

Hundreds of years after Moses penned Leviticus, Herophilos, the celebrated Alexandrian physician of the third century B.C., identified blood as the carrier of disease. However, notice the irony. Centuries earlier, the Bible had presented blood as the carrier of life. And the Bible does not mention even once the weakening, sometimes deadly practice of bloodletting. "The life of every creature is its blood" (Lev. 17:14).

### 7. Urology: Circumcision Is to Be Performed on the Eighth Day[12]

God gave circumcision as a sign of His covenant with Israel. Why was this circumcision to occur on the eighth day after birth?

In 1947 Martin Rosenthal wrote a letter to the editor of *The Journal of the American Medical Association* explaining the best time to perform a circumcision. Babies do not possess adequate clotting factors until five to seven days after birth and therefore can be susceptible to hemorrhaging. Thus circumcision should not be performed until the end of the first week of life in order to prevent the danger of severe hemorrhage. (Today a vitamin K injection is routinely administered after birth to alleviate this danger.)

In other words, the best day to perform a circumcision is on the eighth day after birth.[13] And medical science today still affirms Rosenthal's conclusions.

However, God had told Abraham (some four thousand years previously) the exact day this medical procedure should be done: "For the generations to come every male among you who is eight days old must be circumcised" (Gen. 17:12). The Bible proves to be true even in this medical matter.

### 8. Public Health: Policies Are Needed

For forty years Moses grew up in Pharaoh's court during the writing of ancient Egypt's most significant medical book. In 1536 B.C. *The Papyrus Ebers* became the "bible" of medical books, the recognized world standard, because of Egypt's position as world leader.

This medical volume presents hundreds of medical remedies

including drugs made of "lizard's blood, swine's teeth, putrid meat, stinking fat, moisture from pig's ears, milk goose grease, asses' hooves, animal fats from various sources, excreta from animals . . . human beings, donkeys, antelopes, dogs, cats, and even flies."[14]

Moses knew all these accepted medical practices and potions (actually "quack cures"). Yet as the one chosen by God to be the deliverer at the Exodus, the one through whom God gave the Law, the one who established hundreds of directives regarding health and sanitation, never did Moses recommend these so-called "remedies"; he never mentioned even one of them.

Moses, under God's direction, established laws instructing the people:

- to never eat animals that died of natural causes (Lev. 7:24),
- to destroy contaminated objects (Lev. 11:33; 15:12),
- to isolate or quarantine those who are sick (Lev. 13:4),
- to burn used dressings and contaminated clothing (Lev. 13:47–54),
- to rid a house of any mold (Lev. 14:34–47),
- to wash clothes and bathe after touching someone with an infection or touching the bed of someone with an infection (Lev. 15:11).

Today the public health policies of Moses are totally compatible with public health policies of the modern, civilized world.

As you can see, there are many fields of study in which the Bible shed insight and wisdom years, *even centuries*, before scientists or doctors made their discoveries. Not only has the Bible proved time and time again to be true and reliable, it stands out as a Book like no other because it is the very Word of God!

As the apostle Paul made clear, one reason God gave us His Word is so that we might have *hope*, hope in the guaranteed assurances of His promises. Romans 15:4 says, "Everything that was written in the past was written to teach us, so that through endurance and the encouragement of the Scriptures we might have *hope*."

## 9. Oceanography: Water Paths/Ocean Currents Exist in the Sea[15]

For thousands of years scientists knew nothing about sea lanes and ocean currents. Therefore they drew no water charts for sailing lanes.

Then in 1839, when Dr. Matthew Maury, the father of modern oceanography, became ill, his son began reading the Bible to him. Astonished at hearing Psalm 8:8, he asked to hear it again. As a result he spent several years charting the paths of the seas—the currents of the ocean—which became the basis for the first textbook of modern oceanography, *Physical Geography of the Sea*.

However, this scientific truth had been revealed in the Bible much earlier by David in the tenth century B.C., referring to "all that swim the paths of the seas" (Ps. 8:8).

### 10. Hydrology: Precipitation and Evaporation Cycles Exist[16]

For thousands of years scientists understood the reality of rain clouds that resulted in rain. Yet hydrology—the science of water and the water cycle—was not understood. Unknown was the hydrologic cycle. Then in the first century B.C. Marcus Vitruvius described a philosophical theory—though limited—in which rain falling in the mountains infiltrated the earth's surface, which led to streams and springs in the lowlands.

But it wasn't until the fifteenth century that Leonardo da Vinci presented an accurate picture of the hydrologic cycle. In essence, water on earth moves in a cycle through different pathways and at different rates. For example, the evaporation of ocean water produces clouds—clouds drifting over land produce rain—rainwater flows into lakes and rivers—water in lakes and rivers evaporates back into the atmosphere or eventually flows back into the ocean. And the cycle continues.

However, this scientific cycle had been revealed in the Bible approximately three thousand years prior. The book of Job explains the work of God in this way: "He wraps up the waters in his clouds, yet the clouds do not burst under their weight. . . . He draws up the drops of water, which distill as rain to the streams; the clouds pour down their moisture and abundant showers fall on mankind. . . . Who cuts a channel for the torrents of rain, and a path for the thunderstorm, to water a land where no man lives, a desert with no one in it, to satisfy a desolate wasteland and make it sprout with grass?" (Job 26:8; 36:27–28; 38:25–27). The "who" in the last sentence is the One who invented the cycle in the first place—the One who actually recorded the cycle in His Word.

## 11. Genetics: All Living Things Reproduce After Their Own Kind[17]

In 350 B.C. Aristotle presented the theory of spontaneous generation (life appears out of nonlife)—a theory that the scientific world accepted for thousands of years. Scientists theorized that frogs originated out of slime pools and insects out of rot. Then in 1862, with the invention of the microscope, Louis Pasteur totally disproved spontaneous generation. And three years later Johann Mendel developed what is now the universal law of heredity.

However, thousands of years earlier, in the fifteenth century B.C., the first book of the Bible presented the same law of heredity, verifying that all living things were created according to their own kind. "God created the great creatures of the sea and every living and moving thing with which the water teems, according to their kinds, and every winged bird according to its kind" (Gen. 1:21).

## 12. Epidemiology: Public Sanitation Is Essential

Today no civilized society would allow human dung to be dumped into our public streets. Yet until the end of the eighteenth century body waste lined filthy, unpaved streets. As a result, putrefied stenches hovered over towns like dark, ominous clouds ready to rain their terror of death.

The doctors of that day continually faced deadly epidemics of cholera, typhoid, dysentery, and similar illnesses. The medical doctor who wrote the book *None of These Diseases* states, "It was a hey-day for flies as they bred in the filth and spread intestinal disease that killed millions."[18]

However, if they had merely applied a short, biblical remedy given some three thousand years earlier in the book of Deuteronomy, most of the catastrophic diseases, epidemics, and plagues would have been eradicated. "Designate a place outside the camp where you can go to relieve yourself. As part of your equipment have something to dig with, and when you relieve yourself, dig a hole and cover up your excrement" (Deut. 23:12–13).

## A MOTHER'S FORGOTTEN GIFT

When the book *God's Smuggler* was published in 1968, Brother Andrew became a household name overnight in the Christian community. The book chronicles his adventures while ministering to churches behind the Iron Curtain at the height of the Cold War.

As the shadow of Communism fell over Eastern Europe and the Soviet Union, believers were frequently persecuted. They lost their jobs, their homes, and their families. They suffered physical abuse, imprisonment, and even death.

Andrew, the son of a poor Dutch blacksmith, knew he had to help. He quickly learned there was one thing the besieged believers needed above all else—Bibles! They needed the living, life-changing Word of God.

Many times over the years Brother Andrew himself risked arrest, imprisonment, and beatings to bring the comforting light of God's Word to the suffering church in some of the world's most "closed" countries. To him, the Bible was far more than a book. It was a living promise and a tangible expression of God's plan for us. He wrote:

> The message we proclaim is one of victory through Christ. We win! Because we know what is going to happen, the rest and assurance we radiate will attract many people to hear our proclamation. But that means we must walk closely with God and stay grounded in His Word.[19]

Delivering Bibles to hope-starved people became Brother Andrew's calling. Yet his story really began years earlier when *he* was the one in desperate need of hope.

At seventeen, Andrew suffered a common ailment among young men—restless boredom. He dreamed of adventure, travel, and excitement and longed to leave rural Holland for good. He decided his best chance was to join the Dutch army, which was then waging a bloody war against insurgents in Indonesia.

Before he left, Andrew's mother gave him a small Bible. He dutifully promised to read it but then buried it at the bottom of his duffel bag. Shortly thereafter, he was sent to fight the Communists.

Once in Indonesia, his idealistic fervor quickly wore off. The brutal reality of routine killing was not what he'd imagined. In response he hardened his heart and became daring in combat to the point of recklessness. He fought hard, drank hard, and fully expected to die in the jungle.

But God had other plans. Andrew was shot in the ankle, bringing his career as a soldier to an abrupt end. He narrowly escaped amputation but learned he'd probably be in pain for the rest of his life and would never walk again without a cane.

He later recalled, "I had always seen myself going out in a blaze of contempt for the whole human farce. But to live—and crippled!—that was the meanest fate of all. My great adventure had failed."[20]

During this dark time, a fellow soldier found Andrew's forgotten Bible among his things and brought it to him at the hospital. In two and a half years, Andrew had never once opened it. Even then it lay on the table beside his bed, untouched.

One day he asked a nun who cared for him why she and the other sisters were so cheerful all the time. He vividly remembers her delightful answer: "Why, Andrew, you ought to know the answer to that . . . It's the love of Christ."

> When she said it, her eyes sparkled, and I knew without question that for her this was the whole answer.
>
> "But you're teasing me, aren't you," she said, tapping the well-worn little Bible where it still lay on the bedside table. "You've got the answer right here."[21]

Finally, out of boredom more than curiosity, Andrew began to read the Bible. He read the Gospels straight through, "catching dimly their terrible significance," as he said. *Could all this really be true?* he wondered.

As Andrew lay in bed, he devoured God's Word. Questions poured out of him in a flood of doubt mingled with a hunger for truth. Many months later, back in Holland, Brother Andrew completed the spiritual journey he had begun in the Indonesian jungle. Yes, he concluded, the Bible was true—every single word of it.

It was a momentous decision that would affect thousands of people whose only source of light were the Bibles Brother Andrew loaded into his aging Volkswagen and smuggled across dangerous borders. Brother Andrew brought the light of God's Word to the darkest corners of the world.

## WHAT A LIGHT CAN DO

Think back to Carlsbad Caverns. There you stand, alone in the darkness, with no clue how to retrace your steps to safety. If a lamp was suddenly handed to you, how would that change the circumstances in your subterranean setting? What would the light do? It would *overcome* the darkness and illuminate your way to safety. It would give you hope and end your desperation.

In 1968 the Soviet army invaded Czechoslovakia. While a stream of refugees waited at the border to get out of the country, Brother Andrew packed his car with *Russian* Bibles and headed in. He gave them to Czech believers who ran a terrible risk by passing them out to Soviet soldiers, along with the message, "God is love, and God loves you." Brother Andrew later recalled:

> I later received reports from several cities that within ten days, the Soviet leaders had to recall and replace the entire Russian occupation army! They had become completely demoralized. I have to believe that the love and the Bibles shared by Christians played some part in their withdrawal. After all, the Bible, the Word of God, changes people. And changed people change the situations around them.[22]

You would be hard-pressed to come up with a better picture of light overcoming darkness, of the love of Christ overcoming the lust for power and oppression. Just as light would show you the way out of the Carlsbad Caverns, there is no pitch-black circumstance in your life upon which God's Word cannot shine and restore hope.

## Anchoring Your Hope:
## A Map to Navigate By

Imagine you've planned a trip to a part of the country you've never visited before. You hear it is a tropical paradise . . . beautiful . . . bountiful . . . well worth the journey. However, between here and there lies a vast, treacherous area with no landmarks for guidance. Deadly obstacles are hidden from view. Severe storms can throw you off course. Countless others have set out before you . . . never to return.

But the most significant problem is this: You have no map! Nonetheless, if you are determined to go, consider this: How much would you be willing to pay for an accurate map? What would you give to pinpoint where to find the pitfalls? What would it be worth to know which paths lead to safety and which to disaster? What would you give to get firsthand advice from those who have gone before you?

I already know the answer: *a lot*!

Now you have a small taste of what it was like to be a European mariner at the dawn of the Age of Discovery. Standing on shore and contemplating sailing out into the churning, choppy waters of the Atlantic Ocean had to have been a harrowing experience. Any shred of tangible information was treated like a golden key for unlocking the great mysteries of the deep.

Even as early as the sixth century B.C., when Darius the Great ruled the Persian Empire, mariners were recording details about landmarks and coastal features in written records called "*peripli*." Sea charts, which historians of cartography consider the first true maps ever made, did not appear until the 1300s when captains "first laid down any considerable part of the earth's surface from close, continuous, and what we may call scientific observation."[23] They became known by their Italian name, *portolano* or "harbor guides." These early maps preserved the collective experience of generations of sailors, for the benefit of all.

Today maps are as valuable as ever. Modern mariners have volumes of information at their disposal—detailed data about depth levels, currents, weather histories, and forecasts. No sea captain would venture an ocean voyage without the best maps available.

Facing the future for your own life could feel like looking out on a vast expanse, where tropical storms and hurricanes can stir up at a moment's notice. What hope is there that you will safely reach the other side to experience the abundant life God has promised? The answer is, none . . . if you set sail without the map that He has already provided for your journey. Proverbs 16:25 (ESV) says, "There is a way that seems right to a man, but its end is the way to death."

We have at our disposal the inspired written testimony of those who have gone before us. Their words, inspired by the Spirit of God, identify the treacherous rocks beneath the surface and point the way to the sometimes difficult route we must take, but it's a route that is always right.

At times we find ourselves at the crossroads, and we want to go the right way. This is what the Lord says: "Stand at the crossroads and look; ask for the ancient paths, ask where the good way is, and walk in it, and you will find rest for your souls" (Jer. 6:16).

When you are searching for hope, look no further than the map of God's Word. The insights and inspiration offered there will lead you to the abundant life Jesus promised. Let this be your prayer: "Guide me in your truth and teach me, for you are God my Savior, and my *hope* is in you all day long" (Ps. 25:5).

Without His map, you not only lose your way in life, but you will also lose something vital along the way: *hope.*

# 9

# KNOWING HOW TO NAVIGATE

## HOPE IN THE POWER OF PRAYER

---

*Prayer:*
*The Disastrous Dive—Redeemed*

---

It is easy to spot people who have recently fallen in love. They exude uncommon joy and energy.

Think back to when it first happened to you. Maybe you couldn't stop humming contentedly to yourself or were prone to giggling out loud for no apparent reason. You were suddenly less irritable and more forgiving. The world radiated a soft, warm glow you'd never noticed before. The sky was bluer, the moon was fuller, and life was sweeter than ever.

As William Shakespeare once wisely wrote of being in love, "It adds a precious seeing to the eye."[1]

How many stories, songs, and poems have detailed this mysterious alchemy of romance? Too many to remember! Yet few manage to trace the electrifying energy we feel to its truest source and give it a proper name.

I think lovers can light up a room mostly because they possess something that is rare and priceless in a dark and lonely world—*new hope* . . . being wanted, accepted, and no longer alone—in the present, anticipating sharing a life, raising a family, and growing old together in the future.

One way new lovers express and confirm this hope is by *talking and listening* until their voices nearly give out and their ears nearly fall off! They pour out their deepest dreams and most frightening fears.

Their words are like wires carrying the current of love and hope back and forth between them.

Many new believers in Christ possess the same sort of giddy exuberance. I remember when I entered into a life-changing relationship with Jesus. The Word of God came alive, the songs of praise blessed me, the discovery of His infinite love and grace gave me long-awaited *hope*!

## PRAYER: GOD'S LOVE LANGUAGE

In addition, I *prayed* not out of obligation but because I couldn't help it. I had a Companion, a Champion, a Guide to navigate me through the stormy gales that consistently swept through our home.

Having begun to grasp, though tentatively, that I was truly loved, forgiven, and no longer alone, my newfound hope became a mainstay for my life . . . my peace in the middle of the storm.

Yet for most people, the fire of new love eventually cools. Routine and familiarity gradually replace intimacy and excitement. It is natural for relationships to mellow with age, but some become imperiled by the subtle distancing that sets in.

When this happens, it's easy for heart-to-heart talking to dwindle. As communication breaks down, so does hope that the relationship can deliver what people once believed it could for a lifetime.

Likewise, for some Christians prayer slowly becomes synonymous with duty and discipline . . . having to rise early, getting sore knees, and whipping up fervor we don't always feel. Most come to believe prayer is the province of extraordinary saints and mystics: Elijah fed by ravens, John the Baptist and his life of solitude in the desert, and even Jesus alone in the wilderness for forty days. It is yet another obligation we must try, and frequently fail, to fit into our brutally busy lives.

Often when our sense of hope is under siege and the intimate nearness to God we once enjoyed seems like an irretrievable memory, the reason is remarkably simple: We've stopped talking to Him. Naturally our enemy eagerly exploits this rift in our relationship. Samuel Chadwick put it this way:

> The one concern of the devil is to keep Christians from praying. He
> fears nothing from prayerless studies, prayerless work, and prayerless

religion. He laughs at our toil, mocks at our wisdom, but trembles when we pray.[2]

Why? Because consistent conversation with God renews the exquisite experience of having an intimate love relationship—the bursting, aching sense of being fully alive and complete.

Perhaps this is what the apostle Paul was getting at when he said, "Be joyful always; pray continually; give thanks in all circumstances, for this is God's will for you in Christ Jesus."[3]

Clearly, God intends for our communication with Him to be filled with enthusiasm, anticipation, and delight. The Creator of the universe, our Father in heaven, longs to have intimate conversations with us and to develop the closest possible relationship.

Let the magnitude of that fact sink in for a moment. If that doesn't inspire you to hope, then I fear nothing will.

## SCIENTIFIC PROOF THAT PRAYER WORKS

We have assurance from God's Word that our prayers are heard by our heavenly Father and acted on according to His will. That should be enough to convince us that prayer is *always* the wise and reassuring strategy for all of our troubles, large or small.

But here's more good news: Several credible research studies by physicians and scientists have demonstrated a direct correlation between prayer and healing. Researchers have designed studies using accepted academic standards and protocols to prove what the Bible has said for centuries: Prayer is effective.

One of the earliest such studies was conducted by Dr. Randolph Byrd, a cardiologist and former University of California professor.[4] For ten months Dr. Byrd evaluated 393 patients who were admitted to the coronary care unit at San Francisco General Hospital.

A computer randomly assigned each patient to one of two groups. The first group had 192 patients that would receive prayer. The second group had 201 patients that would *not* receive prayer.

To meet the most rigid criteria for clinical medical experiments, this was a randomized, double-blind study in which the patients did not know to which group they had been assigned; neither did their attending physicians or their nurses. Likewise, those enlisted to pray did not know any of the patients personally. Instead home prayer groups throughout the United States were recruited from the Christian faith, and each was given the patients' names and physical conditions.

Although no instructions were given on how to pray, every person in the group was asked to pray daily for numerous patients. Ultimately five to seven people prayed regularly for each patient.

What were the results? The statistics were staggering. Among other findings, those who received prayer on a regular basis:

- Were more than five times less likely to require antibiotics. (Just three of the prayed-for patients needed antibiotics, in contrast to seventeen of those not prayed for.)
- Were less than half as likely to suffer congestive heart failure. (Only eight of the prayed-for patients were diagnosed with congestive heart failure, compared to twenty of those not prayed for.)
- Were more than four times less likely to suffer cardiopulmonary arrest. (This affected three of the prayed-for patients, compared to fourteen of the patients not prayed for.)
- Were more than four times less likely to contract pneumonia. (Just three of the prayed-for patients were diagnosed with pneumonia, in contrast to thirteen of the patients not prayed for.)
- Were almost three times less likely to undergo major surgery before discharge. (Only five of the prayed-for patients underwent major surgery, in contrast to fourteen of the patients not prayed for.)
- Were twelve times less likely to need an artificial airway attached to a mechanical ventilator. (None of the prayed-for patients required intubation, in contrast to twelve of the patients not prayed for.)

Additionally Dr. Byrd found that the prayers of those living hundreds or thousands of miles away from San Francisco were no less effective than the prayers of those praying in the Bay area. Thus distance was not a factor—dedicated prayer was.[5]

## WHEN PRAYERS ARE NOT ANSWERED

The evidence provided by Dr. Byrd's study and similar studies also mirrors our personal experiences with answered prayers. Sometimes our requests are not granted in the way we would like. As a matter of fact, in certain categories of this double-blind study the results showed no appreciable difference between the two groups.

This affirms that prayer holds no absolute guarantee that the request will be granted. Indeed, the apostle Paul prayed three times for the "thorn" in his flesh to be removed, but it wasn't.[6]

Then there's Jesus. Just after the Last Supper, the Lord went with His disciples to pray in the Garden of Gethsemane, knowing He would soon be arrested and put on trial. The prospect of His imminent crucifixion was excruciating.

He told Peter and the others, "'My soul is very sorrowful, even to death; remain here and watch with me.' And going a little farther he fell on his face and prayed, saying, 'My Father, if it be possible, let this cup pass from me; nevertheless, not as I will, but as you will'" (Matt. 26:38–39 ESV). We know, of course, that Jesus' petition was not granted . . . he was indeed crucified.

If those two central figures in the New Testament—the apostle Paul and the Son of God—made specific requests to God the Father that were not granted, you can be assured we will also have requests that are not granted. In spite of this, the Bible says you are to "present your requests to God."[7]

Additionally we are told to be Christlike. How did Jesus pray? What was the last key phrase in His prayer? ". . . nevertheless, not as I will, but as you will." Jesus made His request and then placed Himself in the hands of His sovereign, all-knowing Father. He expressed His own will and then surrendered His own will, putting the Father's will above His own.

## PERFECT . . . PERMISSIVE . . . PREVAILING

Our hope can be tested when the storms of life sweep over us, and we wonder, *Can this really be God's will?* I generally use three words in an attempt to describe the "will of God"—*perfect*, *permissive*, and *prevailing*. When we understand the different aspects of God's will, we too can know that His plans for us are always superior to our own.

*God's perfect will.* God has an ideal plan that is always pleasing and good. An example is that God desires for everyone to repent of sin, accept Christ as Savior, and spend eternity in heaven. Paul wrote, "Do not conform any longer to the pattern of this world, but be transformed by the renewing of your mind. Then you will be able to test and approve what God's will is—his good, pleasing and perfect will" (Rom. 12:2).

*God's permissive will.* God permits each person to exercise free will . . . even in opposition to His perfect will. God created people not as robots who have no ability to choose but as humans with the ability to choose independently of God.

For example, God's permissive will is that everyone has the option of choosing right or wrong, spiritual life or spiritual death, blessing or cursing. As Scripture says, ". . . choose for yourselves this day whom you will serve. . . . But as for me and my household, we will serve the LORD" (Josh. 24:15).

*God's prevailing will.* God's plans cannot be thwarted, and His ultimate purposes are achieved because He is sovereign. This means, for instance, that God's prevailing will is to grant full forgiveness and a home in heaven to all who repent of their sins and trust in Jesus Christ as their Lord and Savior. "Many are the plans in a man's heart, but it is the LORD's purpose that prevails" (Prov. 19:21).

God indeed has His perfect will. However, He also gives people free will by allowing each of us to go against His perfect will. But the good news is, the hope you are given by God is not based on other people or circumstances, on what is chosen or not chosen.

God gives His people certain hope, which means that regardless of the choices other people make and regardless of the severity of the storms in your life, if you choose to do His will, He will work out His prevailing purposes for you and will ultimately give you peace that passes all understanding.

I personally know the disappointment, confusion, and heartache that can come from wondering why God's will sometimes doesn't align with our own will. I vividly recall the fall day in 1998 when I learned my beloved mother had terminal cancer. Oh, how we prayed for healing! But just a few months later, by Thanksgiving, Mother was in the hospital, with eyes that would not open. She had to be fed by family members and medical staff. Moreover, she was on so much medication that she couldn't communicate with anyone.

Around that time I felt a strong sense of urgency to ask the cancer specialist to take my mother off the high doses of medications she was taking. He responded that she would rapidly decline and we would lose her within weeks. I earnestly sought the Lord's leading and continued to feel prompted by Him to take this course of action.

Finally, the physician agreed to eliminate the medications and then incrementally reintroduce them. Just a day or two later I gathered with four others around Mother's bedside, praying. I could hear my brother, Ray, talking to the doctor out in the hallway.

A split second after the two entered the room, Mother sat up and called out, "Well, well, well . . . it's been so long!" She was as bright and perky as ever. To me it was confirmation that my prayers and petitions for God's leading had been answered.

And there would be further confirmation. My mother lived lucidly and alertly for several more months. That extra time with her was precious, and she continued to be a testimony for the Lord until the day she finally went to be with Him.

My point is this: It was not God's will that Mother be healed of cancer. The Lord did not grant that specific request made by the countless people who interceded on her behalf, myself included. I don't know why, and, honestly, I was heavyhearted because of it.

But God did answer other prayers along the way, like the one mentioned above. And I rest in the assurance that God's will was indeed accomplished, for my every prayer included the phrase that Jesus uttered: "Yet not what I will, but what you will." When we pray with this attitude and perspective, we will know beyond a doubt that we are right in the center of God's will.

## THE PRACTICE OF PRAYER

When loving communion with God is the object of your prayers, the details of how and where and when you pray will take care of themselves. It is a mistake to apply too many rules to the process. Too much head knowledge about prayer only gets in the way.

Even so, the following commonsense pointers, which would enhance any relationship, remind us that God is a *person*, and prayer is nothing more than conversation with the One you love.

*Be present.* Brother Lawrence was a seventeenth-century French monk who worked in the kitchen of a monastery in Paris. Details of his life are recorded in a little book called *The Practice of the Presence of God*.

Brother Lawrence believed that prayer was not a special activity we engage in at special times or only in "sacred" places. For him it was a state of being, the constant awareness that God is present in all things.

> His prayer was nothing else but a sense of the presence of God, his soul being at that time insensible to everything but divine love; and that when the appointed times of prayer were past, he found no difference, because he still continued with God, praising and blessing Him with all his might, so that he passed his life in continual joy.[8]

He realized that because God is present at all times and is as near as our own thoughts, conversation with Him has no obvious beginning or end. Brother Lawrence refused to divide his life into artificial compartments and deprive himself of intimacy with God.

> The time of business . . . does not with me differ from the time of prayer; and in the noise and clatter of my kitchen, while several persons are at the same time calling for different things, I possess God in as great tranquility as if I were upon my knees at the blessed sacrament.[9]

Time you spend behind closed doors in devoted prayer is wonderful and necessary. Just don't be fooled into thinking prayer is always above or beyond your daily life.

It is available to you when you're stuck in traffic, doing laundry, paying bills, or preparing dinner. God is always present and ready to talk. You can be too.

*Be real.* In Mark Twain's *The Adventures of Huckleberry Finn*, Huck finds himself in a moral quandary. He says:

> I made up my mind to pray, and see if I couldn't try to quit being the kind of a boy I was and be better. So I kneeled down. But the words

wouldn't come. . . . It warn't no use to try and hide it from Him. . . . Deep down in me I knowed it was a lie, and He knowed it. You can't pray a lie—I found that out.[10]

It's a shame that Christians sometimes take a long time to discover what Huck realized right away: When you are struggling with one of life's storms, you might as well tell it like it is. God already sees what you would hide.

He knows you are jealous of your coworker's promotion ahead of you. He knows you think your husband might be unfaithful. Why not be honest about how angry or afraid you are? What do you gain by pretending?

If you want to discover the true power of prayer and the true depth of God's love for you, stop telling Him only what you think He wants to hear. You can't shock Him or disappoint Him. Speak the truth to Him:

- "I'm depressed, and I don't know if I want to keep living."
- "I don't want to be a parent anymore."
- "I know I should give up this bad habit, but I really don't want to."

When you pray, be honest. With nothing to hide, you have nothing left to lose by trusting God. Hope begins the moment you give yourself the freedom to be who you are, warts and all, before your loving heavenly Father, confessing your faults to Him and trusting Him to continue to make you into the person He wants you to be.

*Be thankful.* Sometimes we fail to find intimacy with God because our prayers are filled with nothing but our own concerns and requests. In other words, we forget that our interaction with God must flow both ways in order to thrive.

This is not because God "needs" something from us (although we have seen how fervently He *wants* our love). No, it is simply that self-obsession stifles any conversation and eventually stunts any relationship.

That's because in order to give thanks, we must momentarily take our eyes off of ourselves and our problems. Taking stock of His goodness restores lost perspective and reminds us that no matter how rough the seas become, we are securely anchored in Him.

*Be quiet and listen.* Sometimes we think God will be most impressed by an uninterrupted stream of chatter. God is a great listener, but He has plenty to say as well. Many of the problems you bring to Him really do have practical solutions you can know right away. The indwelling Holy Spirit makes it possible to hear His voice with divine clarity and insight you can trust.

When you pray, take time to be still and receptive to God's wisdom.

Charles Haddon Spurgeon wisely wrote, "Because God is the living God, He *can* hear; because He is a loving God, He *will* hear; because He is our covenant God, He has bound himself to hear."

In moments of pain and despair, this is what you need to know to restore your hope: God is willing and able to hear you. Always.

The only uncertainty is this: Are you ready to speak and listen to Him as your Lord, your lover, and your friend? Will you pour out your heart to Him with no pretense? Will you give Him thanks and praise Him for who He is and all He has done? Can you be still in every moment and listen to His loving guidance?

If the answer is *yes*, then hope is sure to be yours again.

"Speak, Lord, for your servant is listening" (1 Sam. 3:9).

# Anchoring Your Hope:
## The Disastrous Dive—Redeemed

At age seventeen Joni had everything going for her—an attractive personality, good looks, and natural athletic ability. She was a tennis player and swimmer, and her physical gifts distinguished her as a true athlete.

But that would all change one hot July afternoon in 1967 when she darted and dashed about in cool waters . . . for the last time.

A self-described risk-taker, Joni positioned herself for a refreshing dive, jumped, and in an instant her body was rocked from head to toe. It was a tragic miscalculation . . . the water was far too shallow. Her head hit bottom, and her neck snapped on impact, leaving Joni paralyzed in all four limbs.

The months that followed were filled with dismay and depressing adjustments to life in a wheelchair . . . and the realization that she would never again do all the physical activities she'd enjoyed before the accident. She found herself having suicidal thoughts, even asking friends to help her end her life.

Thankfully, she had brought to her teen years a Christian faith that had been nurtured in childhood. She admits that her faith was not strong at the time of her accident, but God moved in her life and caused the kind of security in Him that would sustain her through countless challenges.

And there were plenty of daunting disappointments too. She and her family and friends prayed many times for miraculous healing. At one point she decided to attend a healing service. She had hoped to *walk away* from the healing service, but instead she was *whisked away*.

That day Joni Eareckson Tada, wheelchair-bound but holding out hope for a miracle, believed her moment had come.[11] At some point during the service, perhaps while testimonies were shared or choruses were sung, she surely would sense a powerful surge permeating and restoring her body, prompting her to walk away from her wheelchair *forever*.

But the words of an usher soon dashed expectations, not only for Joni but also for about forty others in wheelchairs or on crutches who were hoping for healing. "Let's escort you all out early so as not to create a traffic jam," he directed as other ushers joined in to assist in the exodus.[12]

It was a very solemn stream of individuals who left the arena that day. The service droned on behind them, and Joni remembers thinking, *Something's wrong with this picture.*[13] Another moment of hopefulness had been dashed.

After years of praying for healing and wrestling with Scripture, Joni has found peace and a resolute commitment to the lordship of Jesus Christ in her life. "Suffering is that good sheepdog, always snapping at my heels and driving me into the arms of my Shepherd. For that, I am so grateful. I am so grateful."[14]

Joni is the founder of Joni and Friends, a ministry geared toward facilitating the evangelizing and discipling of people with disabilities.

Surely this courageous woman asked the questions all of us would ask: *Why did this happen to me? Why did God allow it? Why didn't He protect me or heal me?*

From our earthly perspective, we can't know why it was God's will for Joni to experience such a tragedy. But one thing we do know: He has used the experience to speak through Joni in a marvelous and miraculous way. Through the outreach of her hands-on ministry, books, speaking engagements, and daily radio broadcasts, she has brought encouragement and God's love to millions upon millions of people around the globe.

"I'd rather be in this wheelchair knowing Him than on my feet without Him," Joni resolutely declares.[15] But these are not words that roll easily off her tongue. They are couched with grace . . . and grit . . . uttered from decades of pain and anguish in wrestling with the reality of life in a wheelchair, life totally dependent on Him and on family, friends, and colaborers. And it is this same mobile chair that propels Joni before the throne of God like nothing else. For only *there* can she find the strength to deal with her circumstances day by day, and sometimes second by second.

> Let us then approach the throne of grace with confidence, so that we may receive mercy and find grace to help us in our time of need. (Heb. 4:16)

## PART THREE

# The Benefits of Hope — Guaranteed

# 10

# A WRECK RECLAIMED

## HOPE IN THE GIFT OF GRACE

---

*Grace:*
*Finding Hidden Treasure*

---

John Newton (1725–1807) was raised by a devoted Christian mother who longed for her only son to become a preacher.[1] But she died while Newton was still a child, and he eventually followed the example of his sea captain father into a sailing life.

Newton initially had highbrow hopes and joined the Royal Navy, but he didn't like the rigid discipline, so he abandoned ship. Later he was flogged and eventually discharged.

The dishonorably discharged Newton then headed to faraway regions, where he could do whatever he wanted to do, and ended up on the west coast of Africa working for a cruel slave trader.

Newton's life during that period bore the appearance of a modern prodigal son: "a wretched looking man toiling in a plantation of lemon trees . . . clothes had become rags, no shelter and begging for unhealthy roots to allay his hunger."[2] After more than a year of such treatment, he managed to escape in 1747.

Inheriting his father's sea legs, Newton spent a good bit of time at sea, and during one particular severe storm Newton was saved. As waves crashed and swept across the deck of the ship, Newton was tucked away flipping pages, enthralled with what he was reading in Thomas à Kempis's *The Imitation of Christ*. During this life-threatening voyage, Newton gave his life to Christ.

Despite his newfound faith, Newton served as captain of a slave ship for the next six years, but he increasingly came to abhor slavery and later crusaded against it. Initially he was sharing about Christ in whatever vacant building he could find. Later he trained for the ministry and was ordained in the Anglican Church. Known as the "old converted sea captain," Newton attracted large audiences. He not only had a changed life through Christ . . . his life was also anchored in Christ.

The traditional hymns of the day did little to stir Newton's heart. So he began writing his own hymns (many of them autobiographical in nature), including the most beloved hymn of all time, "Amazing Grace!" This indeed was his story.

> Amazing grace! How sweet the sound
> That saved a wretch like me!
> I once was lost, but now am found;
> Was blind, but now I see.
>
> Through many dangers, toils, and snares,
> I have already come;
> 'Tis grace hath brought me safe thus far,
> And grace will lead me home.

After this slave trader received a transformed life, he wanted everyone to experience salvation "by [God's] grace . . . having the hope of eternal life."[3] Newton also collaborated to produce the standard hymnal of evangelical Anglican churches, which for the next century continued to be reprinted in England and in the United States.

As an elderly man, Newton needed to retire because of his declining health and failing memory. He readily admitted, "My memory is nearly gone, but I remember two things: That I am a great sinner and that Christ is a great Savior!"[4]

Down through the centuries, no one knows how many people have been inspired and have received hope through the hymn "Amazing Grace." The guaranteed *hope* that this "great sinner" had in his "great Savior" has impacted innumerable lives throughout the world.

John Newton knew he had absolute security. He had an anchored life. In the fourth verse of this famous hymn, he presents the great security of God's hope:

The Lord has promised good to me,
His Word my *hope* secures;
He will my Shield and Portion be,
As long as life endures.

## WHAT'S SO AMAZING ABOUT GRACE?

As John Newton learned, hope is the end result of the mercy of God being expressed through the grace of God. God's mercy—His magnificent and magnanimous mercy—is the springboard from which His amazing grace reaches out to save helpless, hopeless people . . . whoever they are, wherever they are, whatever they have done.

In His mercy He saves us from the death we deserve, and in His grace He gives us what we don't deserve—eternal life, His Holy Spirit, and rock-solid hope through Jesus Christ. Simply defined, mercy is not getting what we *do* deserve (death) and grace is getting what we *don't* deserve (eternal life and the hope it brings).

> [God] saved us, not because of righteous things we had done, but because of his mercy. He saved us through the washing of rebirth and renewal by the Holy Spirit, whom he poured out on us generously through Jesus Christ our Savior, so that, having been justified by his grace, we might become heirs having the hope of eternal life. (Titus 3:5–7)

Nothing in our finite world prepares us to fully comprehend the infinite grace of God given to us through the sacrificial death and resurrected life of His Son. His forgiveness applies equally to every sinner and every sin, no matter how grievous, how heinous, how seemingly unforgivable!

If you have put your trust in Jesus Christ, God declares you forgiven and makes His power available to you for a victorious hope-filled life. Period.

We each have to personally accept Jesus Christ—this amazing gift of God's grace—as the only rightful Savior and Lord of our lives in order to receive and see His transforming power in our lives.

Accepting Jesus as Lord means allowing Him to rule and reign in our lives. It means giving Him authority over our minds to teach us how to think as He thinks, over our wills to direct us how to act as He acts, and over our emotions to cause us to feel as He feels. God does not save us just so we can live with Him someday in heaven, but so that Jesus, through the Holy Spirit, can live *in* us today on earth.

We are not only destined for a future life in a sinless heaven but for a present victorious life in a sinful world. The abundant life Jesus promised us can be ours today! It is there for the taking, but it comes wrapped in the clothes of humility and requires submission to the Spirit of God in our lives.

Submitting to the lordship of Jesus Christ in your life means letting Him live His abundant life through you here and now by allowing His Spirit to make you into the person He created you to be—a person accurately reflecting His character, His attitudes.

Even then you may need to attempt to repair the damage your sins have done to others and to yourself. But Jesus died on the cross for all of our sins to give us life . . . eternal life . . . so that if we will give Him control of our lives, we will be forgiven for *all* of our sins at that very moment.

That's truly amazing. Sometimes it seems *too* amazing for those of us who feel our sins are unpardonable. It's important to remember what grace actually is—*unmerited, undeserved favor*. It is a gift and simply can't be earned. For some of us, that flies in the face of justice unless we remember that God meted out justice over two thousand years ago when Jesus shed His blood on a cross.

He died in full payment not only for our sins but also for the sins of the whole world. He did that so that He can now mete out mercy and grace to all who accept His sacrifice and receive the justification of their sins.

Grace is the very essence of our faith. Without it the Christian life makes no sense at all, and we are totally without hope. Grace is a mystery we must simply acknowledge and accept . . . an undeserved blessing that is ours for the taking . . . and sharing.

> Because of his great love for us, God, who is rich in mercy, made us alive with Christ even when we were dead in transgressions—it is by grace you have been saved. And God raised us up with Christ and seated

us with him in the heavenly realms in Christ Jesus, in order that in the coming ages he might show the incomparable riches of his grace, expressed in his kindness to us in Christ Jesus. For it is by grace you have been saved, through faith—and this not from yourselves, it is the gift of God. (Eph. 2:4–8)

## MAKE TRUTH YOUR LIFEBOAT WHEN DROWNING IN GUILT

Too often the amazing truth of God's grace is overshadowed by the dark clouds of our own guilt. If you're in that boat, it's important to know that guilt is not always your enemy . . . nor is it always your friend. Distinguishing good guilt from bad guilt is vitally important.

To do this, first ask: Is your guilt the loving prod of God, used to convict, correct, and conform your character . . . especially when you've gone astray? Or do you battle vague feelings of shame, disgrace, and disgust no matter how many times you try to deal with your sin?

You see, true guilt is your friend . . . a godly companion who whispers truth and motivates you to turn and be free. But false guilt is a relentless foe . . . an inner enemy that wounds you with sorrow—worldly sorrow—a superficial sorrow that ends in death!

> Godly sorrow brings repentance that leads to salvation and leaves no regret, but worldly sorrow brings death. (2 Cor. 7:10)

Here is how to distinguish between the two types of guilt and some guidance for dealing with each:

*True guilt* is the result of having committed wrong. This good guilt is designed by God to bring genuine sorrow over your wrong choices—not just sorrow that you got caught—and to convince you to take responsibility for your part in the negative consequences that occur in your own life or in the lives of others.

Like traveling south and then all of a sudden realizing, *I'm heading the wrong direction* (which I have done), good guilt is actually designed by God to turn you around so you will be all He created you to be and will do all He created you to do.

He who conceals his sins does not prosper, but whoever confesses and renounces them finds mercy. (Prov. 28:13)

*False guilt* is the feeling of unjustified self-condemnation. This bad guilt involves being overly self-judgmental, overly responsible, overly conscientious, or overly sensitive when you have done no wrong or when you have repented and turned away from your wrong. False guilt may be the result of having other people put you on an unjustified guilt trip.

It can also be the impetus for extreme self-denial, demonstrated by overly serving others (being a people pleaser), displaying low self-worth, and having emotional blocks that produce negativity and hopelessness.

When guilt immobilizes you, the following steps will help you discern false guilt, thus allowing your heart to embrace the truth of God, which will free you to embrace the *hope* of God. Jesus not only wants us to be set free, but He also tells us what will set us free: "You will know the truth, and the truth will set you free" (John 8:32).

*Discern the truth by honestly asking . . .*
- "Do I have true guilt or false guilt?"
- "If I have truly repented of my sin, why do I still feel guilty?"
- "Why am I struggling with hopelessness?"
- "Am I in any way responsible for my lack of hope?"
- "Does guilt make my feelings of hopelessness worse?"
- "If my guilt were removed, would I feel hopeless?"

If our hearts do not condemn us, we have confidence before God. (1 John 3:21)

*Once you discern the truth about your guilt . . .*
- Sincerely ask God to forgive you for any sin causing you to experience true guilt and to forgive you for holding on to any false guilt.
- Steadfastly place your hope in Jesus Christ, choosing to believe in His personal acceptance of you and in His total forgiveness of your sins.
- Saturate your mind with Scriptures that encourage you to receive God's complete acceptance of you.

There is now no condemnation for those who are in Christ Jesus. (Rom. 8:1)

Listening to countless callers to HOPE IN THE NIGHT, I've learned there are few things more tragic than being shanghaied in a sea of false guilt long after God has extended us freedom through His forgiveness.

Such was the case with Ron. I'll never forget his despairing voice, his downcast spirit, his dejected heart the night he called.

*Last Saturday I was driving for my company, and a little boy and his family were crossing the street. I hit him, and he went underneath the van. He was five years old. . . . He died.*

Ron, I'm so very sorry—not just for the family but also for you. How are you processing this?

*I have a hard time sleeping. I go to counseling . . . but the impact . . . the screaming and all the blood that poured out from the back of his head . . . he was five years old. It's the worst cry I've heard in my life.* [Ron's voice began to crack.] *I had to back the van off him. I can't forget the impact . . . and there was nothing I could do.*

I hear you, Ron, and I know that if you could have done anything, you would have saved that child. Is that right?

*Yes. He'd just bought a gift for his mom for Mother's Day, and he and his sister and another guy were crossing the street, and I had the green light and just like slow motion I saw his hand breaking away from his sister . . . and the impact . . . and then my big van on top of him. I've been reading and the Bible says "Thou shall not kill."*

I'm hearing that you are feeling a sense of blame.

*Yes.*

Ron, my heart goes out to you. You have endured a trauma that few people could even begin to fathom. I want you to look with me at the intent of the Scripture you mentioned, "Thou shall not kill." The word "kill" here indicates a choice, an act of the will to murder. You had no intent to murder anyone. Is that correct?

*June, I didn't want to kill anybody. And that innocent, happy little boy. . . .*

Of course not. You see, Ron, God looks at your heart. What happened was not an act of your will. You didn't make a decision to kill a boy.

*Is his spirit in heaven now? What happens to children when they die?*

Scripture tells us that David's infant son died, and David made the statement, "I will go to him, but he will not return to me" [2 Sam. 12:23]. The point is, David was a righteous man, so he was saying that when he died he would go to his child in heaven, meaning the child would already be there. Also, that child would have no sorrow, no pain, no heartache. There will be heartache, certainly, for the family.

And I understand why you are having difficulty right now. If that had happened to me, I, too, would be heartbroken over the loss of that child's life and the impact on the family. Even though the child would be in heaven, I would ache for his family. Do you understand what I'm saying?

*Yes. I was going to go into ministry, and I was going to join a pro-life organization, and I'm going to be an uncle in October. I don't have the courage to even hold a child now. It hurts so bad every time I see one walk past when they get out of school.*

Ron, right now you're going through a grieving process. And that is perfectly normal and even beneficial. You don't want to stop or short-circuit the process. You're going to get over the grief, but what I don't want you to have is false guilt. You did not make a choice that ended up in the loss of life for another person. Did police ticket you for your role in the accident?

*No, the witnesses said it wasn't my fault. But that doesn't make me feel any better. I haven't driven since then. I can't drive anymore. How could I?*

I appreciate that you have a compassionate heart. But it is not going to be a blessing from God for you to live with false guilt, nor an honor to that boy's life if you just quit driving—quit living—forever. Let's say that God's will is for you to go into ministry.

*Yes.*

Now here is this five-year-old boy in heaven. Do you think he would want you not to go into ministry . . . not to be a part of saving the lives of children? You are pro-life and you are wanting to save lives, right?

*That's right.*

That probably means that you will have to travel. Is that right?

*Yes.*

And do things on behalf of unborn children. That is honoring life. That is saving life, as opposed to shutting down. Does God want you to totally shut down?

*I don't know.*

I believe you *do* know, Ron! God does not want you to totally shut down. God has a good plan in store for you, not only something to do, but a way to learn from this. What I'm hearing is, you are valuing life all the more. So let this be a positive springboard toward discovering, "How can I choose to do something in honor of this boy?" This boy made a mistake. Is that correct?

*Yes.*

He ran into you. You did not cause this. So it does not bring honor to the memory of this child for you to live in false guilt. You need to say, "Lord, I want to honor this boy through the way I live my life." Does shutting down in false guilt honor his life?

*No.*

So you need to tell yourself the truth. Jesus said the truth will set you free. Many, many, many children die. The question is: Do we honor those children by what we do in their memory? You have that opportunity before you now.

I had the privilege of leading Ron in prayer as he humbly asked God to heal his heart and to use his life to save and serve others.

As the call ended, Ron's newfound relief from false guilt—and resolve to live in the freedom that truth brings—was palpable. He had allowed the forgiveness of God to work in him, enabling him to forgive himself for the accident.

His heart was still full of sadness and sorrow over the tragedy that so profoundly touched many lives, including his own, but he had a stronger resolve to value life and to be used of God to honor the life of that little boy.

God's grace is inexplicable. It is not what we deserve. But when we receive it with humble hearts and pass it on to others with mercy and compassion, it can change the world.

Hope is never more elusive than when you believe you don't deserve it. You think your mistakes and shortcomings are exceptional and deserve an extra helping of misery and punishment. God says otherwise.

Frances Roberts, in her classic devotional *Come Away My Beloved*, envisions Jesus' tender message to His children when she writes, "Draw near to me without spoiling the preciousness of our fellowship with self-condemnation."[5]

When you feel burdened by the weight of your own failings, think like He does: Forgive yourself.

## Anchoring Your Hope: Finding Hidden Treasure

An article from the *Billings Gazette* reported that an extraordinary treasure had been discovered on the beaches of Florida. Joel Ruth came across 180 near-mint-condition silver coins. These Spanish coins were from a Spanish fleet of about a dozen ships that were destroyed by a hurricane in 1715.[6]

Then 289 years later another hurricane uncovered a portion of this treasure that had washed ashore. It took Hurricane Jeanne, a devastating tropical storm responsible for some of the worst destruction in Florida's history, to bring that slice of shoreline back to where it had been years before. The storm exposed an impressive treasure to the one who went looking for it.

From a spiritual standpoint, look at what the Lord so often does: He'll allow a storm in your life to expose some hidden treasure. Are you willing to look for it? Imagine this: In the midst of a painful storm He might prepare you for a personal ministry of mercy that you will later discover. After a costly crisis He could be uncovering coins of compassion for you to pick up and ultimately share with others. Through a severe, scary tsunami you may experience the grace of God like never before, which you can then give to others.

What personal hurricane have you experienced? What did you learn from it? As a result, what treasure do you have that you would otherwise not have?

The apostle Paul wrote, "We have this treasure in jars of clay to show that this all-surpassing power is from God and not from us."[7] "Jars of clay" refers to what people see when they look at us—our weak, mortal bodies. "This treasure" is the light of Christ inside us shining through our cracks. The light of Christ shines the love of Christ and also shines His light rays of empathy, grace, compassion, and mercy.

And what happens when we possess this surpassing power? "We are afflicted in every way, but not crushed; perplexed, but not driven to despair; persecuted, but not forsaken; struck down, but not destroyed" (2 Cor. 4:8–9 ESV).

You are promised the *gift* of grace. This means at times you will be pressured by people but will not be *depressed*. You will be at wit's end but not at hope's end. You will be persecuted by people but not persecuted by God. You will be knocked down in life but not knocked out.

Now read this slowly: "It is all for your sake, so that as grace extends to more and more people it may increase thanksgiving, to the glory of God" (2 Cor. 4:15 ESV).

What is the reason for your hope? God's gift of grace. He forgives you for all of your failures, sustains you through all of your storms, and reveals treasures after your trials.

# 11

# CHARTING YOUR COURSE
## HOPE TO PINPOINT YOUR PURPOSE

---

*Purpose:*
*Taking a Different Tack*

---

Not long ago I led a conference for several hundred single men and women. At one point I distributed index cards and asked them to write down their most pressing problem, something they've struggled to overcome but continues to challenge them.

The most common response was not surprising for a large group of singles—loneliness. The second response *was* surprising to me and to many of the event sponsors—feeling useless.

Many of those young, eager, bright, spiritually minded men and women felt a lack of purpose and direction. They had no strong sense of calling, no vision of their destiny, no anticipation of what lay ahead. They had no wind in their sails.

Instead they felt adrift on the stagnant sea of life, at the mercy of the meaningless currents of world opinion and world values that swirled around them. Honestly, I was quite shocked and saddened by the large percentage of these young people who were clueless as to their precise mission on earth.

But maybe I shouldn't have been surprised. Countless people today feel aimless, unfulfilled, and purposeless. Consequently their hope for abundant life in this present life has run amuck. They may be involved in lots of worthwhile activities, even serving the Lord diligently, but they sense a void, as though they should be investing their lives in something bigger, more important.

## THE PURPOSE QUESTION

Years ago when I was totally absorbed in serving teenagers as a youth pastor, a respected church leader stopped by my office to chat. I treasured such visits and was always eager to soak up whatever wisdom he had to share. After a while he asked, "So, June, what's your purpose in life?"

Caught off guard by the question, I thought for a moment, then said, "Well, I want to do whatever God wants me to do."

"That's great," he persisted, "but what's your *purpose*?"

I'm sure I looked a bit befuddled, because I was. I didn't understand exactly what he was asking of me, so he graciously came at it from a different angle.

"What brings you the most joy?" he asked. "When you're doing what God wants you to do, what thrills and delights you more than anything else? That's where you'll find your purpose."

We sat in silence for several minutes as I seriously pondered the question. Finally I replied, "I feel most alive, most used by God, when I'm teaching and I see light bulbs go on in people's heads. It's when I'm communicating spiritual truths, and they *get it*. I could be talking to one person or a thousand . . . it doesn't matter. I feel most energized and excited . . . like the Holy Spirit is successfully working through me . . . when I tell people about God and His Word and I know it's sinking in down deep where it can change lives."

That brief conversation had a huge impact on my life and the hope I have in what God is doing in me, to me, and through me. During the subsequent years I have more clearly defined what I consider to be God's calling on my life.

My *inner* purpose is to gain as much wisdom as I possibly can from spending time with God and studying His Word and rubbing shoulders with people who possess godly wisdom. My *outer* purpose is to share the transforming truths of Jesus Christ through both the teaching and the application of God's Word. And I want to do that with as many people as I possibly can.

I've come back to these statements over and over, and they have helped keep me on track. Since I am notorious for taking on more than

I can reasonably accomplish and for saying *yes* to more things than I should, sometimes to the chagrin of all who work with me, keeping these purpose statements in sight helps me recalibrate my priorities.

Doing so has pressed me into some tough decisions as I've felt the need to resign from several boards and pass up some marvelous opportunities. Many *good* things can lure us away from the *best* thing God has for us . . . the purpose God wants to accomplish through us and the hope He wants to instill in us along the way.

The British pastor, evangelist, and writer F. B. Meyer wisely pointed out:

> Nothing is more disastrous than aimless drift, for God endows each person for a distinct purpose. Sometimes, there may come a lucid moment when there flashes before us a glimpse of the lifework for which we were sent forth. Still other times, we may look ahead as into a veil of mist, and we walk forward by faith, believing that the fog will lift.
>
> Believe it: God will unfold our life purpose, if not in a flash then step by gradual step. Let us go steadily forward, counting on our Almighty Guide to supply the needed grace, wisdom, and strength. He will not desert the work of His own hands! What plan God has in mind for you, He will provide all to see it through to completion.[1]

What brings *you* the greatest joy in life? What makes you feel more alive and energized than anything else? What puts wind in your sails, bolsters your confidence, and enhances your hopefulness? The Lord does indeed have plans for you, to give you a future and a hope.

It is your job—through prayer, study of the Scriptures, godly counsel, meditation and introspection, and a bit of trial and error—to discern what exactly God is calling you to do. I like the way Pastor Kirbyjon Caldwell puts it: "There are two great moments in a person's life: the moment you are born and the moment you realize *why* you were born."[2]

Discovering your purpose is not about the *what* questions but the *why* questions. Everyone can say what they're doing (working at a software company, teaching Sunday school, playing on the softball team, and so on), but when pressed, most people can't tell you precisely *why* they're doing those things.

## THE POWER OF PROPERLY DIRECTED PURPOSE

Both were *powerful* men, *prominent* leaders, *progressive* change-makers
. . . they both changed the history of the world. They were both exceptional orators . . . changing minds, hearts, and lives. They were both *heralded as heroes* . . . literally impacting millions of people. Whatever they set about to do sent ripple effects around the world.

They both possessed *purpose-driven lives* . . . but each took a distinctly different course. The apostle Paul was driven by a *divine* purpose . . . Adolf Hitler by a *diabolical* purpose. The apostle Paul found *all* meaning in life tied to one person, his Lord and Savior Jesus Christ. All his striving, struggling, serving was for the glory of another. Self was sacrificed . . . for the cause of Christ.

Hitler, too, found all meaning in life tied to and wrapped up in one person—*himself.* "I shall become the greatest man in history." So said the infamous Führer. "I have to gain immortality even if the whole German nation perishes in the process."[3]

Adolf Hitler sought to fulfill his purpose in life first by serving his country as a corporal in World War I. After the war, his strong sense of patriotism led him in the direction of politics, and he penned *Mein Kampf,* which translated means "My Struggle," a two-volume set dictating his ideology.

Surrounding himself with a handful of like-minded men, he became leader of the National Socialist German Workers Party (the Nazi Party) and was named Chancellor of Germany in 1933 and Führer in 1934. Emerging as a dominant political force, his influence soon became global, garnering him the title "Man of the Year" by *Time* magazine in 1938.

But Hitler's greatest source of significance did not come from titles or top billing on the world stage. His sense of self-worth was rooted in what he believed was a divine mandate, a mission given to him by God Himself.

Hitler wrote, "My feeling as a Christian points me to my Lord and Savior as a fighter. It points me to the man who once in loneliness, surrounded only by a few followers, recognized these Jews for what they were and summoned men to the fight against them."[4]

Hitler sought death for the Jews, but the apostle Paul sought to bring them life, *eternal life*. His was a labor of love, and he anguished over their repeated rejection of the gospel message.

At one point it appeared as if both men were headed for the same destiny . . . arm in arm, on the same course of corruption. Hitler wanted to kill the Jews, and Paul, when he was previously known as Saul, wanted to kill the Jews who had become Christians . . . to kill the early church . . . to squelch its impact, dragging off its people to prison. All the while, both men truly believed they were serving God.

As a young man, Paul thought he was fulfilling his purpose in life when he "began to destroy the church" (Acts 8:3). A zealous Pharisee in the early days of the church, he went house to house dragging off men and women who were followers of Jesus Christ and putting them in prison. He stood by and watched while Stephen, the first Christian martyr, was stoned for his faith, consenting to his death.

But his campaign against Christians ended when he had a conversation with the risen Christ and his real purpose in life began. "Still breathing out murderous threats against the Lord's disciples" (Acts 9:1), Paul was traveling to Damascus and was on the outskirts of the city when "a light from heaven flashed around him" (Acts 9:3).

Jesus appeared to Paul and revealed that in persecuting the church, Paul was in reality persecuting Jesus. Later, after Paul experienced the transforming work of Christ in his life, Jesus said of him, "This man is my chosen instrument to carry my name before the Gentiles and their kings and before the people of Israel" (Acts 9:15).

The apostle Paul was flogged for his faith, beaten for his beliefs, imprisoned for his purpose, put in chains for his choice. Clearly he had chosen to follow Christ no matter what.

Hitler's colossal rise to power in the 1930s came crashing down in 1945. But before all was said and done, the damage incurred from a relatively brief stint of power was devastating. Just one life, far outside of God's purposes, had tremendous impact . . . tragic impact.

The notorious Nazi regime not only provoked World War II, but Hitler ordered the killing of approximately six million Jews as well as five million others he deemed racially inferior or politically dangerous.

The savagery ended with Hitler's suicide as the Allied Forces poured into Nazi-occupied territories.

Life . . . and death . . . came dishonorably to Hitler, who was preoccupied with his own glory and couldn't bear to see it wane.

When Paul got off the path of persecution and onto the road to righteousness, only then did he *truly* begin to serve God. He became the leading theologian of the apostolic age and was labeled "Apostle to the Gentiles."

His life was characterized by fruitful labor for the Lord—evangelizing, teaching, discipling, praying, planting churches, and sending weighty doctrinal letters to God's people, who at times he felt the need to rebuke. But Paul always reinforced his deep love and concern.

Hitler was preoccupied with power, *and not just political power*. While he publicly proclaimed himself a Catholic, it is widely documented that Hitler owned a number of books on the occult and was discipled by Dietrich Eckhart, leader of the Thule Society, also known as the German Brotherhood of Death Society.

On his deathbed Eckhart had the following to say about Hitler: "Follow Hitler! He will dance, but it is I who have called the tune! I have initiated him into the 'Secret Doctrine,' opened his centers in vision, and given him the means to communicate with the Powers."[5]

And concerning the astronomical rise in SS membership from three hundred in 1929 to fifty-two thousand in 1933, Hitler attests, "The hierarchical organization and the initiation through symbolic rites, that is to say without bothering the brains but by working on the imagination through magic and the symbols of a cult—all this is the dangerous element and the element I have taken over."[6]

Hitler was eager to rise to the call of an impoverished German nation weary of sluggish democratic reforms and wanting to revive its sense of national pride. He embraced references like "Messiah" and "Savior," although it was political leadership that put Germany back on the map.

Hitler revived a dismal economy, reclaimed the Rhineland, lowered the crime rate, built freeways, and eliminated unemployment. And for all these "miraculous" accomplishments, *he was adored,* ushering in the diabolical and distinctive salute of Nazi worship: "Heil, Hitler!"

Enmeshed in lofty titles, sacrilegious symbols, and adulation, Hitler announced it was time to begin a new religion in order to instigate a system of beliefs that would strengthen the German people, *not weaken them as Christianity had.*

Talk of mercy and forgiveness sapped Germany of its strength, according to Hitler, and in his religion there would be no fear of a bad conscience or death. People "would be able to trust their instincts, would no longer be citizens of two worlds, but would be rooted in the single eternal life of this world."[7] Hitler felt himself on a divine mission to save Germany and in chilling blasphemy proclaimed: "What Christ began . . . I will complete."[8]

And for Hitler, the end *always* justified the means. "The victor will never be asked afterward whether he told the truth or not. In starting and making a war it is not might that matters, but victory."[9]

Yet, long before, the apostle Paul had spoken these words: "They perish because they refused to love the truth and so be saved. For this reason God sends them a powerful delusion so that they will believe the lie" (2 Thess. 2:10–11).

Two purpose-driven lives with incredible comparisons and contrasts! Paul went on a missionary journey during which he invited people to surrender their lives to Christ. Hitler occupied foreign territories where he forced people to surrender their lives to him. How opposite their aims!

Paul strived to bring life to the Jews. Hitler strived to bring death to the Jews. Paul spread love. Hitler spread hate. Paul recognized his purpose as glorifying God. Hitler saw his purpose as glorifying self. Paul died honorably as a martyr for the Lord. Hitler died dishonorably by the act of cowardly suicide.

The comparison between these two towering historical figures shows one thing for sure: Those who see themselves as the center of their life purpose are headed in a disastrous direction. But those who place God at the center of their purpose will be used by Him in great ways and will be led by Him on a grand adventure.

## CLAY POTS PUT TO GOOD USE

God wants to utilize our talents and in so doing give us a sense of purpose and fulfillment. He wants us to have a properly directed, life-giving purpose. Still, many people I speak with feel like they are nothing special and therefore couldn't be used by God in any great way. Scripture makes it clear that God uses ordinary, humble folks who are surrendered to Him.

A motif running through both the Old and New Testaments is that of God as the potter who shapes and molds the clay, us, to utilize as He deems best. As Isaiah said, "O LORD, you are our Father; we are the clay, and you are our potter; we are all the work of your hand" (Isa. 64:8 ESV).

And Paul wrote to Timothy, "In a large house there are articles not only of gold and silver, but also of wood and clay; some are for noble purposes and some for ignoble. If a man cleanses himself from the latter, he will be an instrument for noble purposes, made holy, useful to the Master and prepared to do any good work" (2 Tim. 2:20–21).

## DISCERNING YOUR CALL

If you are committed to being totally sold out to Christ and being fully utilized by Him, that's the beginning of recognizing God's plan for your life and rekindling hope in your heart. Collectively, we are all created:

- *To be like God in true righteousness and holiness.* "Put on the new self, created to be like God in true righteousness and holiness" (Eph. 4:24).
- *To let God be the true King of our hearts.* "Seek first his kingdom and his righteousness" (Matt. 6:33).
- *To be the image-bearer of God.* "God created man in his own image, in the image of God he created him; male and female he created them" (Gen. 1:27).
- *To be conformed to the character of Christ.* "Those God foreknew he also predestined to be conformed to the likeness of his Son" (Rom. 8:29).
- *To bring glory to God.* "Everyone who is called by my name . . . I created for my glory . . . I formed and made" (Isa. 43:7).

We were also individually created with a specific plan for our lives. To understand the nature of God's specialized work in your own personal life you need to do the following:

*Realize that God has a personal and unique purpose for your life.* The mission He calls you to is tailor-made just for you, and He has gifted you with all you need to accomplish it. "We are his workmanship, created in Christ Jesus for good works, which God prepared beforehand, that we should walk in them" (Eph. 2:10 ESV).

*Realize God's promise to reveal His purpose for you.* He doesn't play games with us, and finding your way in life is not a matter of hide-and-seek. God wants you to reach your full potential, and He's provided the means for you to discover how. "I will instruct you and teach you in the way you should go; I will counsel you and watch over you" (Ps. 32:8).

*Realize the power of prayer to reveal God's purpose.* As we listen to the Spirit and humbly ask for direction, we will, in time, discern His calling. "Do not be anxious about anything, but in everything by prayer and supplication with thanksgiving let your requests be made known to God. And the peace of God, which surpasses all understanding, will guard your hearts and your minds in Christ Jesus" (Phil. 4:6–7 ESV).

*Realize that God will faithfully use your spiritual gifts, yielded to Him, to accomplish His purpose for you.* We all have different talents and abilities, and we need to make sure our ambitions align with our aptitude. "We have different gifts, according to the grace given us. If a man's gift is prophesying, let him use it in proportion to his faith. If it is serving, let him serve; if it is teaching, let him teach; if it is encouraging, let him encourage; if it is contributing to the needs of others, let him give generously; if it is leadership, let him govern diligently; if it is showing mercy, let him do it cheerfully" (Rom. 12:6–8).

*Realize the value of asking practical questions of godly counselors.* Tap into the wisdom and experience of those you trust. God has placed people in your life to serve as guides, advisers, and encouragers. "A wise man listens to advice" (Prov. 12:15 ESV).

Once you've taken these foundational truths to heart, you can take the next step of identifying God's specific calling. You can:

*Discover God's leading through your circumstances.* Carefully evaluate which situations in your life have brought you success and which have brought failure, excitement or boredom, fruitfulness or frustration. God uses all the experiences in your life—whether positive or negative—to steer you in the right direction. "Many are the plans in the mind of a man, but it is the purpose of the LORD that will stand" (Prov. 19:21 ESV).

*Discover opportunity through obedience.* "If you are willing and obedient, you will eat the best from the land" (Isa. 1:19).

*Discover how to wait for God's timing.* All of us want to receive our marching orders and begin fulfilling them *right now*. But sometimes God is preparing us and grooming us for bigger and better things, so He tells us to be patient and to continue diligently serving Him where we currently are. "Wait for the LORD; be strong, and let your heart take courage; wait for the LORD!" (Ps 27:14 ESV).

*Discover the essential goals for your life.* Define the goals that will help you achieve your purposes, goals that are specific and reachable, beneficial to but not dependent on others for success, in line with God's will, and made with deadlines for completion.

Nearing the time of His crucifixion, Jesus was questioned by Pilate. In the course of that inquisition Jesus said, "For this purpose I was born and for this purpose I have come into the world" (John 18:37 ESV). Christ had the kind of single-minded focus and assurance of His calling that we should strive to attain.

If you are unclear about God's specific purpose for your life, spend ample time in the upcoming weeks asking Him to reveal His plan for you. Think about your greatest source of delight and gladness, and consider how you could best serve the world by putting to full use your God-given talents, passions, and skills.

Ask God to prepare you, lead you, and open doors for you so that you can fulfill the mission to which He has called you. Your sense of hopefulness, fulfillment, and bright outlook on life are sure to soar as you, by faith, work to achieve the unique purpose God has set out for you.

And consider this: No one who has ever lived, is living now, or will ever live can accomplish *your* purpose. This is something only *you* can do . . . something only *God* can do through you.

The one who calls you is faithful and he will do it. (1 Thess. 5:24)

# Anchoring Your Hope: Taking a Different Tack

In this age of abundant energy, it's hard to believe that our ancestors once explored and colonized every corner of the world using nothing but *the power of the wind*. With timber masts and canvas sails, they ventured across vast oceans, defying storms and reefs in the harshest climates. As long as a steady wind blew, there was no point on the compass where they couldn't go.

Well, almost. There is one direction the best sailing ship can never ever go. From the beginning, every sailor at sea learns this simple fact: *You cannot sail straight into the wind!*

To understand why, think about a flag flying on a windy day. If you hold a flag straight into the wind, it flaps and flutters as the wind blows by, but it cannot catch any of the wind like sails do on a sailboat. However, to get the wind to work for you, tightly hold the cloth steady in the wind *at an angle*.

Sailors have a unique vocabulary to describe the relative positions of a boat to the wind (called "points of sail"):

- *In irons*: A sailboat facing directly into the wind might as well be locked in irons . . . because it isn't going anywhere. The sails will only flap in the wind.
- *Close-hauled*: A craft is close-hauled if the sails are trimmed tightly and moving as near upwind as possible without landing in irons. If the helmsman steers too close into the wind and the sails start "luffing," the boat is said to be pinching.
- *Close reach*: Sometimes called fetching, a vessel in close reach means the sails are anywhere between close-hauled and at an angle of 45 degrees.
- *Beam reach*: This point of sail is when the mainsheet is placed at a 45-degree angle and the boat is moving at right angles to the wind.
- *Broad reach*: A sailboat is in broad reach when the wind blows from behind at various angles, but not from directly behind.
- *Running*: Boats are running when sails are angled at 90 degrees to catch wind blowing directly from the stern, from the rear. While you may think this point of sail is the fastest way to travel (with the wind pushing you from behind), experienced sailors also know this point

of sail is the most dangerous, often referring to it as the "don't go zone." Your running sailboat is less stable, harder to steer, and more susceptible to jibing or capsizing. (A sail that jibes shifts suddenly and dangerously from one side to the other.)

Here's the point: Sailing is the art of getting somewhere on an *indirect* course. Each leg of the journey is called a tack, and an experienced sailor strings them together, tacking in a zigzag pattern that methodically moves the sailboat toward the desired destination. To an uninformed observer, a particular tack often looks like it is tracking too far to the right and then to the left. But that is all part of a systematic strategy to safely arrive at a desired destination, harnessing the power of the wind.

Putting your hope in the Lord during your journey through life requires that same kind of strategic patience. You must keep your eyes firmly on God, trusting Him no matter how often the course of your life changes. Remember, your ultimate destination is accomplishing the purpose for which you were created.

When your hope is in the Lord's plan and purpose for your life, letting Him determine the exact direction—the angle of each tack—your journey will be absolutely secure. The Lord says in Jeremiah 29:11, "I know the plans I have for you . . . plans to prosper you and not to harm you, plans to give you hope and a future." And when you fulfill God's purpose for your life, you will arrive safely in the harbor . . . because He is at the helm.

# 12

# UNTANGLING YOUR KNOTS

## HOPE TO BE FREE . . . BY FORGIVING

---

*Forgiveness:*
*Batten Down the Hatches*

---

Scott was the first to admit he wasn't a perfect father. He'd often given far too much of himself to his work and far too little of himself to his son, Andrew. Looking back, he sorely wished he had scolded less and sympathized more . . . that he'd laughed more and worried less.

Yet for all that, Scott knew he wasn't the worst father in the world either. He genuinely loved Andrew and worked hard to provide a safe and proper home for him. He agonized over every childhood illness and teenage crisis and always wanted the very best for his son. In spite of his flaws, he felt he'd done a pretty good job as a parent.

But when Scott called me one evening during a *Hope In The Night* broadcast, it had been five years since he'd spoken to Andrew. A bitter argument had turned into a nasty fight, and their stubborn anger had opened what seemed to be a colossal chasm of silence and pain between them. It was obvious from the emotional strain in Scott's voice that the memory of that injurious encounter was as fresh in his mind as if it had happened yesterday.

After high school Andrew had gone to college in another city. Scott covered the costs but made it clear he expected Andrew to do his part by studying hard and doing well in his classes. It didn't take long for evidence to start piling up that things weren't going according to plan.

"First he began bouncing checks," Scott told me. "Then he wrecked the car I'd bought for him, apparently during a street race that could have gotten him killed. By the time he came home at the end of his first semester, he was close to being expelled and lucky not to be in jail. To top it off, he looked like he'd had a hangover for four solid months."

When Scott confronted his son, Andrew angrily told him he had no intention of living a life as "pointless and boring" as his father's.

"He said he'd rather die in a gutter than be like me," Scott recalled. "I told him I'd have been better off childless than to have a spoiled delinquent for a son. It was an awful thing to say, I know, but I'd had it."

More venomous words were exchanged, dredging up old conflicts. Andrew left in silence the next morning before either of them could take back what he'd said. Andrew left a note saying he would be dropping out of college and joining the Army. Scott didn't know if he was doing that to exert his independence, sow his wild oats, spite his father, or all of the above.

"I still feel dead inside, like I did that day watching him leave," Scott told me bitterly. "All my hope in God's blessing and protection went out the door with him."

I know from experience that Scott's heartbreaking words speak for thousands of hurting people who struggle to forgive others . . . and themselves. Although God commands us to forgive those who harmed us, just as we have been forgiven, many believers struggle to let go of their pain, their pride, or their intense desire for vindication.

Yet sooner or later it all comes down to a glaring moment of decision: Will we continue to choose slavery to anger, pride, and pain, or will we let God lead us to the freedom of forgiveness? Will we leave our stomachs and our relationships tied up in knots of unforgiveness or work to untangle them? Our physical, emotional, and spiritual well-being as well as the healthiness of all of our relationships depends on our answer.

For Scott, such a moment had finally arrived. The morning of the day he called me, he had received an unexpected invitation to Andrew's wedding in the mail. Tucked inside the printed card was a handwritten note that read, "I'd like you to be here . . . if you want."

"That's wonderful!" I told Scott. "You must feel like the father of the Prodigal Son who looks up and sees his boy coming over the horizon!"

But for Scott, like so many of us, it wasn't that easy. He had no confidence that the pieces of their shattered relationship could ever be put back together again. Too much time had gone by, he thought, and too much damage had been done. The knots of unforgiveness seemed too tightly woven together to ever be untangled.

"I don't know what to do," he said. "I can't bear to open these wounds again. If I go, what assurance do I have that reconciliation is even possible?"

"That's a legitimate question," I told Scott, "and I wish I could give you that assurance. But reconciliation requires everyone involved doing their part, and there are no guarantees that will happen. The good thing is, Andrew has opened the door for that possibility, which gives you reason to believe it *can* happen and to have hope it *will* happen."

The truth is, without the anchor of hope there is no way we can ever steady ourselves in a raging gale of anger, pride, and pain long enough to forgive someone who has offended us, much less find the strength to untie and heal the knotted relationship. We feel too vulnerable to more pain. We feel like forgiveness and reconciliation are impossible. But when our hope is in God, we know that He is willing and able to repair *any* damage done and to restore *anything* that was lost. Hope is the crucial ingredient that makes it all possible.

Interestingly, people who have read my book *How to Forgive . . . When You Don't Feel Like It* have made more comments about the section explaining the differences between forgiveness and reconciliation than about any other part of the book.

The same is true of our *Biblical Counseling Keys* on the topic of forgiveness. Many people do not understand that forgiveness is not the same as reconciliation.

Forgiveness focuses on the offense, whereas reconciliation focuses on the relationship. Forgiveness requires no relationship. However, reconciliation requires a relationship in which two people, in agreement, are walking together toward the same goal. The Bible says, "Do two walk together unless they have agreed to do so?" (Amos 3:3).

The truth is:

| | |
|---|---|
| *Forgiveness* | can take place with only one person. |
| *Reconciliation* | requires at least two people. |
| *Forgiveness* | is directed one way. |
| *Reconciliation* | is reciprocal, occurring two ways. |
| *Forgiveness* | is a decision to release the offender. |
| *Reconciliation* | is the effort to rejoin the offender. |
| *Forgiveness* | involves a change in thinking about the offender. |
| *Reconciliation* | involves a change in behavior by the offender. |
| *Forgiveness* | is a free gift to the one who has broken trust. |
| *Reconciliation* | is a restored relationship based on restored trust. |
| *Forgiveness* | is extended even if it is never earned. |
| *Reconciliation* | is offered to the offender because it has been earned. |
| *Forgiveness* | is unconditional, regardless of a lack of repentance. |
| *Reconciliation* | is conditional based on the offender's repentance. |

The bottom line is: Forgiveness is a choice that a person makes to not extract payment from someone who has committed an offense against him or her. In no way is it contingent on the offender. You can choose to forgive anyone at any time for anything. Reconciliation, on the other hand, is a choice made by offenders and offended persons alike to do what it takes to lay a new foundation on which to build a new relationship.

It is a joint undertaking contingent on forgiveness being given and received and is dependent on all involved agreeing that reconciliation is God's will. Sometimes it isn't. But in Jonah's story, it was. . . .

## SEEK RECONCILIATION, NOT REVENGE

For centuries the prophet Jonah has held a dubious distinction as one of the foremost biblical characters often pointed to as a *bad* example, a role model *not* to emulate. Anyone who has attended Sunday school or has read a book of famous Bible stories remembers how Jonah went from divine spokesman to discouraged sulker. Instructed by God to travel to the city of Nineveh to warn the wicked people of impending judgment and doom, Jonah heard but did not heed. He said essentially, "Sorry, not me!"

Jonah hopped a ship sailing for Tarshish, which was 180 degrees in the opposite direction from Nineveh. En route a fierce storm arose, and the sailors, fearing for their lives, cast lots and determined that Jonah was to blame. When confronted, Jonah "fessed up" and eventually was tossed overboard, which caused the seas to calm.

Then came the big fish, sometimes called a whale, which swallowed the dog-paddling prophet. Jonah spent three days and three nights inside the stomach of the fish before suffering the indignity (and relief) of being vomited onto dry land. Not surprisingly, when God gave the same orders a second time, Jonah complied.

He went to Nineveh, and lo and behold, the evil people there repented and begged the Lord for mercy. The king issued a proclamation calling for all the people to fast, give up their sinful ways, and plead for God's grace. Indeed the Lord heard their cries and withheld his judgment.

The ending we want is for Jonah to say, "Hooray! Praise God! My preaching and prophesying worked. All of those formerly evil Ninevites will be spared because of the Lord's great compassion." But no. He started grumbling and grousing. He became angry that God did not send down fireballs and lightning bolts from heaven to destroy the wicked people. In fact, he got so distraught that he twice asked God to end his life. "Now, O LORD, take away my life, for it is better for me to die than to live" (Jonah 4:3; see also v. 8).

How could this man go from winner to whiner so quickly? The short answer is that he was much more interested in revenge than in reconciliation. Historians tell us that at the time of Jonah, the Israelites were very proud of their special status as God's chosen people. They basked in the glow of the Lord's favor, and they did not want neighboring countries to experience His blessing.

Jonah, you might say, wore black-filtered glasses. He could see only what was bad and dark and depraved about the people of Nineveh, and he didn't expect them or want them to turn to God and be reconciled to Him by His grace. He wanted them to be ruined, not redeemed.

Before we judge Jonah too harshly, let's admit that we might have done the same thing if we were in his sandals. And in fact we often have similar attitudes toward groups or individuals whom we do not feel are deserving of God's grace and mercy. We want vengeance. We hope for God's justice to come crashing down on their heads. Sadly, we wish they would "get what's coming to them."

As with Jonah, God tells us to go out of our way to show grace, extend an olive branch of peace, and demonstrate divine love. We're to do so even with those who have hurt us and wronged us. God is a God of justice, and He will deal with people in His time and in His way. That's His job, while our job is to seek reconciliation and resolution whenever possible.

When you struggle to heal broken relationships, meditate on the following fundamental reasons for hope:

## WE HOPE IN GOD'S HEALING

Many people, like Scott, say they feel dead inside after suffering a traumatic offense. Believing that healing is out of the question, they haven't the strength, or even the desire, to forgive those who wounded them. That is an understandable reaction to great pain. Yet tragically some people remain in this state of shock for years, even for a lifetime.

What's needed at such times is hope's reviving assurance that "with God all things are possible" (Matt. 19:26). When we cling to that truth in spite of our pain, we remember there is no wound He can't heal and no wrong He can't right. Nothing lies beyond His reach . . . not even death itself.

One day when Jesus was teaching His disciples, a "ruler" approached and knelt before Him. The man explained that his daughter had just died and asked Jesus to "'come and lay your hand on her, and she will live.' . . . And when Jesus came to the ruler's house and saw the flute players and the crowd making a commotion, he said, 'Go away, for the girl is not dead but sleeping.' And they laughed at him. But when the crowd had been put outside, he went in and took her by the hand, and the girl arose" (Matt. 9:18, 23–25 ESV).

Hope doesn't care who laughs or shouts or threatens. Hope knows that when God takes us by the hand, we *rise* . . . no matter what we've suffered. Restored to life by hope in God's healing power, we may also feel the quickening of forgiveness in our hearts, where only bitterness and revenge had been.

I have spoken at many conferences on the topic of forgiveness and have provided a practical illustration that has helped free people from the bonds of bitterness.

Think of a relationship in your life that is troubled or even "hopelessly" broken. Have you ever said, "I want to forgive, but how can I simply let my offender off the hook?" If these words have passed through your lips or even crossed your mind, be assured that you are not alone. That is precisely why you need to know how to handle "The Hook."

Make a list of all the reasons you have for holding a grudge against your offender. Don't be afraid if your reasons sound harsh or petty. Be honest and be thorough.

Now imagine a meat hook around your neck and a burlap bag hanging from the hook in front of you. And imagine that all the pain caused by the offenses against you are dropped into the burlap bag. So now you have hundreds of pounds of heavy rocks . . . rocks of resentment . . . hanging from the hook around your neck.

Ask yourself, *Do I really want to carry all that pain with me for the rest of my life?*

If not, then surrender each offense to God, forgiving the offender and giving the pain to God.

Also take the one who offended you off of your emotional hook and place him or her onto God's hook. As you do, you will restore your hope that God can help you make the relationship whole again, and you will open yourself up to receiving God's healing. Here is a prayer that can help you express forgiveness toward your offender.

Lord Jesus, thank You for caring about how much my heart has been hurt.

You know the pain I have felt because of (*list every offense*).

Right now I release all that pain into Your hands.

Thank You, Jesus, for dying on the cross for me and extending Your forgiveness to me.

As an act of my will, I choose to forgive (*name*).

Right now, I move (*name*) off of my emotional hook to Your hook.

I refuse all thoughts of revenge. I trust that in Your time and in Your way You will deal with my offender as You see fit.

And, Lord, thank You for giving me Your power to forgive so I can be set free.

In Your holy name I pray. Amen.

## WE HOPE IN GOD'S JUSTICE

Many of the stories appearing in books, movies, and on television today depict a culture that values a vigilante form of justice. "Good guys" using deadly force, committing their own crimes in the process, deal with the "bad guys." The message is simple: If you don't administer your own revenge, no one will. If you can't *see* justice being done, you have failed, and the offender will "get away with it."

The psalmist showed us a much better way when he wrote:

To you, O LORD, I lift up my soul;
in you I trust, O my God.
Do not let me be put to shame,
nor let my enemies triumph over me.
No one whose hope is in you
will ever be put to shame,
but they will be put to shame
who are treacherous without excuse.
Show me your ways, O LORD,
teach me your paths;
guide me in your truth and teach me,
for you are God my Savior,
and my hope is in you all day long. (Ps. 25:1–5)

The kind of justice we hand out with a vengeance always causes more harm than good. But when we leave such matters to the Lord, we are freed from the fear of being "put to shame" or left at the mercy of our enemies. We put our hope in His ways and in His paths, making authentic forgiveness and reconciliation possible.

## WE HOPE IN GOD'S PLAN

Scott told me he couldn't imagine what purpose his rift with Andrew might have served. To him the pain was pointless and futile. That's because logic alone is too narrow a lens to allow us to see what God sees. He understands there are things we need to know that we can learn only through hardship. He is willing to let the storms brew and rage in order to prepare us to receive even greater blessings.

In other words, He has a *plan*. "A man's steps are directed by the Lord" (Prov. 20:24).

After we talked, Scott decided to trust God with all the sticky issues of blame and pride and regret he'd been carrying around for years. He went to Andrew's wedding, willing to face uncertainty and vulnerability to more pain. After a few awkward moments together, it was obvious that deep down both men wanted to find the road back to a healthy, untangled relationship.

"There's no question we have more work to do," Scott told me later. "But just knowing I don't have to face it alone makes all the difference."

The precious fruit of our hope in God is the chance to untangle knotted cords of resentment and to restore relationships we thought were lost forever. When we surrender to His healing power, His righteous justice, and His perfect plan, *nothing* is impossible.

## Anchoring Your Hope:
## Batten Down the Hatches

On April 2, 2001, the worst accident in fifty years involving an American fishing boat took place on the Bering Sea. The *Arctic Rose*, a 92-foot commercial fishing trawler, went down in frigid waters 205 miles northwest of St. Paul Island. All fifteen crewmen aboard drowned. No radio call for help was sent.

The Coast Guard began an investigation that lasted nearly three years. Eventually the *Arctic Rose* was discovered 428 feet under the sea, but only one body, that of Captain David Rundall, was found.

Based on an underwater video of the wreck, the inquiry came to certain conclusions. Although the exact cause was not definitively determined, a possible reason for the disaster was discovered. The underwater cameras revealed that several of the ship's doors and hatches had been left open. Since not all the crew members were experienced seamen, more than likely they were not diligent in keeping the ship watertight.

Investigators found that leaving watertight doors open contributed to the sinking of the boat. Waves over twenty feet high struck the boat from the rear and side, sweeping through open doors and hatches. In less than three minutes the boat was flooded beyond recovery, and it sank within eight minutes.[1]

Not all open doors are positive opportunities. Some are doors to disaster. This is certainly true in our lives! One potentially dangerous door we leave open is bitterness. A refusal to shut the door to bitterness can lead to unforgiveness, grievous grudges, and ruined relationships.

Heed the wisdom of the writer of the book of Hebrews: "See to it that no one misses the grace of God and that no bitter root grows up to cause trouble and defile many" (12:15). A seemingly small action, like not shutting the door to grudges, can cause unforgiveness to flood every compartment of your heart and sink your significant relationships. Failing to close those doors can lead to disastrous consequences . . . it can be a matter of life and death.

The Bible leave us with no other option. Colossians 3:13 says, "Bear with each other and forgive whatever grievances you may have against one another. Forgive as the Lord forgave you."

Simply put, to keep from drowning, batten down the hatches to bitterness, resentment, and hatred. Shut the doors and keep them shut!

Then, finally, you will see for yourself that forgiveness will protect you from a watery grave and give you free sailing.

# 13

# YOUR NEXT PORT: PARADISE

## HOPE TO INHERIT HEAVEN

---

*Heaven:*
*When the Seas Will Cease*

---

What is right for you to hope for . . . what is reasonable? And more importantly, what *should* you put your hope in . . . how much do you know?

In *Our Greatest Gift*, Henri Nouwen presents a fascinating parable of hope. He tells about twins, a brother and sister, talking to each other in their mother's womb.

The sister says to the brother, "I believe there is life after birth."

Her brother protests vehemently, "No, no, this is all there is. This is a dark and cozy place, and we have nothing else to do but to cling to the cord that feeds us."

The little girl insists, "There must be something more than this dark place. There must be something else, a place with light where there is freedom to move."

But she cannot convince her twin brother.

After some silence the sister says hesitantly, "I have something else to say, and I'm afraid you won't believe that either, but I think there is a mother."

Her brother becomes furious.

"A mother!" he shouts. "What are you talking about? I have never seen a mother, and neither have you. Who put that idea in your head? As I told you, this place is all we have. Why do you always want more?

This is not such a bad place, after all. We have all we need, so let's be content."

The sister is quite overwhelmed by her brother's response and for a while doesn't dare say anything more. But she can't let go of her thoughts, and since she has only her twin brother to speak to, she finally says, "Don't you feel these squeezes every once in a while? They're quite unpleasant and sometimes even painful."

"Yes," he answered. "What's special about them?"

"Well," the sister says, "I think these squeezes are there to get us ready for another place, much more beautiful than this, where we will see our mother face-to-face. Don't you think that's exciting?"

The brother doesn't answer. He is fed up with the foolish talk of his sister and feels the best thing is simply to ignore her and hope she will leave him alone.[1]

I love that phrase, "I think these squeezes are there to get us ready for another place, much more beautiful than this." Many of us do, in fact, feel squeezed and squelched and squashed. Life has a way of tightening its grip to the point of making us feel suffocated and smothered.

What we are being prepared for, of course, is the world beyond this one. We are being made ready for our eternal home in heaven. The Bible clearly presents the promise of heaven and the transition from here to there: "Now we know that if the earthly tent we live in is destroyed, we have a building from God, an eternal house in heaven, not built by human hands."[2]

Looking forward to our eternal home should bring light to even the darkest circumstances. This is one of the greatest sources of comfort and hope we have, as we cling to the promise of an extraordinary life beyond this life. For the Christian, we know that once we are "away from the body," we will be "at home with the Lord,"[3] the apostle Paul tells us.

When you have an endearing relationship, the thought of losing that loved one can be painful. And then when that loved one is no longer living, sometimes the words spoken aren't accurate.

When my "you-light-up-my-life" friend Sue breathed her last breath, I heard the words "We've lost her." The truth is, Sue wasn't *lost.* Sue knew exactly where she was—she had arrived at the port of paradise . . . she was experiencing the splendors of heaven.

But as believers we must always remember, God is moving us along to our final destination—heaven. What we are being prepared for in this life is the next life.

Those who have the blessed hope of heaven know unfalteringly that death is not the end—it is a transition into an eternal beginning. I discovered some years ago a word picture that is wonderful.

### Death

I'm standing on the seashore.
A ship at my side spreads her white sails
to the morning breeze and starts for the blue ocean.
She's an object of beauty and strength
and I stand and watch her until, at length,
she hangs like a speck of white cloud
just where the sea and the sky
come down to mingle with each other.
And then I hear someone at my side saying,
"There, she's gone."
Gone where?
Gone from my sight, that is all.
She is just as large in mast and hull and spar
as she was when she left my side.
And just as able to bear her load of living freight
to the place of destination.
Her diminished size is in *me*, not in her.
And just at the moment when someone at my side says,
"There, she's gone;" there are other eyes watching her coming,
and there are other voices ready to take up the glad shout,
"Here she comes!" And that is dying.[4]

We can look ahead with great eagerness to the day when we shall arrive at the shores of heaven and at long last see the Lord Himself . . . our Anchor. To those who have served Him faithfully, He will say, "Well done, good and faithful servant! . . . Come and share your master's happiness!"[5]

It is hard to imagine more meaningful words than those, nor could there be a more blessed reward than spending eternity with our

Master, who no longer will need to anchor us through the storms of life because in heaven there are no storms.

## THE CONNECTION BETWEEN HEAVEN AND HOPE

What do you know about heaven? What's your impression of what it will be like? We are given hints and glimpses from Scripture, and we can see that:

- This is your hope: Jesus said, "In my Father's house are many rooms. If it were not so, would I have told you that I go to prepare a place for you? And if I go and prepare a place for you, I will come again and will take you to myself, that where I am you may be also."[6]
- This is your hope: "He will wipe away every tear from their eyes, and death shall be no more, neither shall there be mourning, nor crying, nor pain anymore, for the former things have passed away."[7]
- This is your hope: "In [God's] presence there is fullness of joy; at your right hand are pleasures forevermore."[8]
- This is your hope: "There the weary are at rest."[9]
- This is your hope: "Nothing impure will ever enter it, nor will anyone who does what is shameful or deceitful, but only those whose names are written in the Lamb's book of life."[10]
- This is your hope: "Then I looked and heard the voice of many angels, numbering thousands upon thousands, and ten thousand times ten thousand. They encircled the throne and the living creatures and the elders. In a loud voice they sang: 'Worthy is the Lamb, who was slain, to receive power and wealth and wisdom and strength and honor and glory and praise!'"[11]

Images like these help shape our impressions and fill in parts of the painting, but many important aspects are still hidden from our view. After talking with thousands of people over the years, many of whom were in the midst of terrible adversity, I've become convinced that there is a direct correlation between a person's conception of heaven and the degree of hope they have.

Those with only a vague sense of what heaven will be like and a hazy image of what awaits them often lack a proper perspective of their lives here on earth. The difficulties of life weigh them down because they're focused on the *here and now* and give little thought to the *there and then.*

Conversely, those who have spent considerable time pondering heaven, meditating on it, and formulating a clearer picture of it recognize the thin veil between life below and life above. They acknowledge the Scripture that states, "What is seen is temporary, but what is unseen is eternal."[12] They also understand more fully that their troubles here on earth are inconsequential compared to the glories and delights we'll enjoy forever in heaven.

The apostle Paul assures us, "We do not lose heart. . . . For our light and momentary troubles are achieving for us an eternal glory that far outweighs them all."[13]

Does this mean that those who live in eager expectation of heaven are able to smile their way through the storms of life? No. No one enjoys pain. But when you know for certain you're headed for that final home in heaven, your clear view of eternity gives you a proper perspective for your temporary trials.

When your hope is in heaven, your earthly suffering, though very real and painful, does not become all-consuming to the point of hopelessness. You know that soon enough your tears will be wiped away and your sadness will turn to joy. As the psalmist says, "Weeping may remain for a night, but rejoicing comes in the morning."[14]

Over the years I have sung at numerous funerals . . . some victorious and some tragic. Of all the songs I have sung and have heard others sing, one grips my heart like no other. Apart from the haunting melody, the words of the chorus capture for me what death is like for the child of God. It paints perfectly the picture of what it is like to reach the shores of heaven.

A dear family friend sang this song at my mother's memorial service (and I have requested it for my own). These words touch my heart and stir my hope.

### Finally Home[15]

When engulfed by the terror of tempestuous sea,
Unknown waves before you roll;
At the end of doubt and peril is eternity,

Though fear and conflict seize your soul.
*Chorus*: But just think of stepping on shore and finding it heaven!
Of touching a hand and finding it God's!
Of breathing new air and finding it celestial!
Of waking up in glory and finding it home!

When surrounded by the blackness of the darkest night,
O how lonely death can be;
At the end of this long tunnel is a shining light,
For death is swallowed up in victory.
*Chorus*: But just think of stepping on shore and finding it heaven!
Of touching a hand and finding it's God's!
Of breathing new air and finding it celestial!
Of waking up in glory and finding it home!

Ask people on the street if they want to go to heaven when they die and you'll undoubtedly hear a resounding "yes" from just about everyone. Ask them if they want to go to heaven today and from most you'll hear a resounding "no." They want to *eventually* go, but there are dreams in this life they want to fulfill first.

## DISTORTED IMPRESSIONS

Randomly ask ten people to describe heaven, and you're likely to hear references to harps, pearly gates, clouds, and angels that resemble chubby babies. These simplistic stereotypes show up repeatedly in movies, television shows, cartoons, advertisements, and comedy routines.

What a sad misrepresentation! Such clichéd and shopworn images have become ingrained in our society's collective consciousness, but they couldn't be further from the truth!

Heaven is a place of utter beauty where we will find utter fulfillment. And by the way, in the Bible, when people encountered angels, they didn't find them cuddly, they found them *terrifying* because they are magnificent, powerful, supernatural beings committed to serving our God.

Personally I never really felt the need or even desire to focus on heaven until my mother was ready to go be with the Lord. Then I began thinking of what it would be like for her to be there.

Though I could no longer see her sweet face, I knew she was

face-to-face with Christ her Savior. Now as I think of her and miss her (at times I still have unexpected tears), my greatest comfort of all is knowing she is at home in heaven in the precious presence of God . . . in the presence of her loving Lord. Heaven is sweeter by far, and my mother is there.

Realize, God has astonishing and amazing things in store for you. The Bible tells us, "No eye has seen, no ear has heard, no mind has conceived what God has prepared for those who love him."[16] You're in for an awe-inspiring future! Make no mistake, this is no fairy tale . . . you *will* live amazingly, happily ever after!

## SUFFERING SEAFARERS

For those who feel battered and beleaguered by the storms of life . . . for the hungry, hurting, imprisoned, tortured . . . for those who have few options for improving their lot in this life, hold on, dear ones—the next port is paradise. When drowning in despair it's hard to imagine a better life, but a blessed, eternal life awaits, free of all pain. You're headed . . . *home*. "But our citizenship is in heaven,"[17] Paul reminds us.

On the last page of the final book of The Chronicles of Narnia, some of the children who have gone to Narnia lament that they once again must return to their homeland, the Shadowlands. But Aslan, the lion who represents Jesus, has the best news of all for them.

> Speaking to the children, he said, "You do not yet look so happy as I mean you to be."
>
> Lucy said, "We're so afraid of being sent away, Aslan. And you have sent us back into our own world so often."
>
> "No fear of that," said Aslan. "Have you not guessed?"
>
> Their hearts leaped and a wild hope rose within them.
>
> "There was a real railway accident," said Aslan softly. "Your father and mother and all of you are—as you used to call it in the Shadowlands—dead. The term is over, the holidays have begun. The dream has ended; this is morning."
>
> And as he spoke he no longer looked to them like a lion; but the things that began to happen after that were so great and beautiful that I cannot write them. And for us this is the end of all stories, and we

can most truly say that they all lived happily ever after. But for them it was only the beginning of the real story.

All their life in this world and all their adventures in Narnia had only been the cover and the title page: now at last they were beginning Chapter One of the Great Story, which no one on earth had read, which goes on forever, in which every chapter is better than the one before.[18]

We can't fully know what eternal life will be like or what wonders heaven will hold. But we can be assured that one delight after another awaits us. And there will be no more stormy times . . . only serenity. Truly our hope is in the promise of heaven.

## *Anchoring Your Hope:*
## *When the Seas Will Cease*

One of the most common expressions associated with *hopelessness* is "Things will never change."

When we look around our world today, we see a steady stream of hatred and violence manifested in a myriad of ways. It has been that way since the beginning of history. And now things seem to be going from bad to worse, and society seems destined for moral decay . . . forever.

*Nothing could be further from the truth.*

One of the most common expressions associated with *hopefulness* is "Change is a'comin'," as President Dwight Eisenhower and others have said. And oh, is it ever.

The Bible presents this hope-filled promise: One day all sin will cease, and that means *all sin*. There will be a new heaven and a new earth, and what are characterized as seven evils (death, mourning, weeping, pain, the curse, night, and the sea) will be gone. *The sea?* Yes, in the book of Revelation the apostle John specifically prophesies, "Then I saw a new heaven and a new earth, for the first heaven and the first earth had passed away, and *the sea* was no more" (Rev. 21:1 ESV).

What could this possibly mean? For a literal interpretation, consider these two certainties about our future: We will no longer face the proverbial storms of life, nor will we be in the proverbial "sea of troubles."[19]

While water covers the vast majority of the present earth's surface, according to the Bible that will not be the case with the new earth. But why? Because the sea is often perceived as an opponent to humanity—turbulent, untamable, and terrifying when its great waves thunder and crash. If there is no more sea, there will be no more hurricanes and tidal waves, no more tropical storms and feared typhoons, no more cyclones and tsunamis, all of which have devoured and destroyed millions of lives.

Can you imagine how many lives have been lost at sea, how many drownings from disastrous shipwrecks? If someone sailing alone in the middle of the sea is deprived of help and hope, the untamed waters will swallow the sailor, leaving him to die in its murky depths.

But change is a'comin' . . . and that should give us all a renewed sense of hope. This kind of hope "does not disappoint us"[20] because we will permanently be in God's presence. Pain will cease forever, and peace will reign forever. And we will be at home in heaven . . . at home in our true home . . . for *eternity*!

> He has made everything beautiful in its time. He has also set eternity in the hearts of men. (Eccles. 3:11)

# 14

# WHEN SEA BILLOWS ROLL
## HOPE TO POSSESS PERFECT PEACE

---

*Where Is Your Hope?*

---

Horatio Spafford is not a household name, but this respected lawyer, who experienced unimaginable loss, has long been a shining example of enduring hope.

Before the Civil War, Horatio met his wife-to-be, Anna, in Chicago when she began attending the Bible class he taught at his Presbyterian church. By the year 1871, they and their four young daughters (Annie, Maggie, Bessie, and Tanetta) were living just north of Chicago when the Great Chicago Fire spread as an all-consuming inferno, destroying much of the city.

Unfortunately, many of the Spaffords' real estate properties went up in flames, and while the couple's personal residence was spared, the financial loss was significant.

During the next two years, Horatio and Anna worked tirelessly in relief efforts on behalf of the many desperate and destitute Chicago residents. By 1873 this exhausted couple needed rest and recuperation, so they planned a family vacation in Europe.

Additionally, because the Spaffords were strong supporters and close friends of renowned evangelist D. L. Moody, they planned to assist Moody as he traveled through Great Britain on one of his crusades where they knew countless lives would be changed.

In November 1873 the Spaffords traveled to New York, where they were to set sail aboard the French steamer SS *Ville du Havre*. At the last minute, a business obligation required Horatio's brief return to Chicago. Not wanting to disrupt the family trip, the weary couple decided that Anna and the girls would go ahead of him to France. Horatio would join them shortly.

This practical decision proved to be life-altering.

An English ship, the *Lochearn*, accidentally rammed the large luxury ship on which Horatio's family sailed. Amidst the sound of twisting metal and rushing water, panic ensued. Anna made it to the deck with her four daughters clinging to her.

The ship sank in a mere twelve minutes, claiming the lives of most of the passengers and crew—226 in all. An hour later, rescuers found Anna floating unconscious in the water, a bare plank keeping her afloat. All four girls, however, had drowned.

Long afterward, Anna described the moment when she regained consciousness in the lifeboat. In utter despair she remembered the rushing waters tearing her daughters from her grasp. But a voice seemed to speak to her from within: "You are spared for a purpose. You have work to do."

Several days after the tragedy, the rescue ship arrived in Cardiff, Wales. Anna sent her husband a simple two-word telegram: "Saved alone."

*It can't be . . . all four of my precious girls gone?* The caring, grief-stricken father felt horrified and helpless. Yet even in his agony, even in his anguish, he affirmed his faith. He told a friend, "I am glad to trust the Lord when it will cost me something." And for Horatio the cost was incomprehensible.

Horatio immediately set off to rejoin his heartbroken wife. During the voyage the captain of the ship called him to the bridge.

"A careful reckoning has been made," the captain said, "and I believe we are now passing the place where the *du Havre* was wrecked. The water is three miles deep."

After a time of pensively looking over the watery grave, in the midst of deep sorrow, Horatio began to pen the lyrics of the beloved hymn, "It Is Well with My Soul." The first verse conveys the ocean imagery:

> When peace, like a river, attendeth my way,
> When sorrows like sea billows roll;

Whatever my lot, Thou hast taught me to say,
It is well, it is well, with my soul.[1]

This hymn holds a special place in my heart for three reasons. First, when my father lay in the hospital dying of cancer, the day before he breathed his last breath, this was the last song I sang for him. My personal prayer was that the melody and words would give him peace . . . that sweet peace that "surpasses all understanding."[2]

A few days later I sang "It Is Well with My Soul" at his funeral. And as I sang these words, I distinctly thought back to his eighty-sixth birthday when, for the first time in his life, he prayed to receive Jesus as his personal Lord and Savior. What a difference to have true peace . . . to have peace *from* God and peace *with* God.

As I sang another verse, I applied it to my father.

My sin, oh, the bliss of this glorious thought!
My sin, not in part but the whole,
Is nailed to the cross, and I bear it no more,
Praise the Lord, praise the Lord, O my soul!

The last reason I am so endeared to this hymn involves the many hearts all around the world who have been calmed and comforted by its message of hope. As I think about the hundreds of memorial services where I have been asked (and honored) to bring comfort through a ministry of music, no song has been *more* requested than "It Is Well with My Soul" . . . penned in the midst of pain by a man who desperately needed peace.

A Scripture I have been drawn to for years perfectly reflects this godly lawyer and businessman. "The fruit of righteousness will be peace; the effect of righteousness will be quietness and confidence forever" (Isa. 32:17). Because he was right with God, he had the peace of God.

The part of the hymn that always causes joy to swell within my soul is the very last verse. It contains a glimpse of the hope every authentic Christian has, reminding us of our *guaranteed hope* of eternity in heaven. Notice the words "my faith shall be sight"! We will literally *see* what God planned *firsthand*! It will all be unrolled like a scroll.

And Lord, haste the day when my faith shall be sight,
The clouds be rolled back as a scroll;
The trump shall resound, and the Lord shall descend,
Even so, it is well with my soul.

The refrain repeats this again and again to emphasize this glorious truth.

It is well, with my soul,
It is well, with my soul,
It is well, it is well, with my soul.

The tragic beauty of this classic hymn has drawn countless people to Christ during the darkest times and is made all the more meaningful when people learn of its writer's deep woes.

## WHEN FACING DEATH MAKES A DIFFERENCE

On November 23, 1892, D. L. Moody and his son Will boarded the ocean liner *Spree* at Southampton, England. Moody, Horatio Spafford's admirer and supporter, had just finished speaking at meetings in London, and now he was bound for New York. Foremost in his mind, besides seeing his family and students again, was planning his next year's great outreach campaign for the Chicago World's Fair.

On the third morning of the trip, passengers were startled by a loud crash and a strong reverberation rumbling throughout the vessel. Young Will hurried onto the deck, then quickly returned, yelling, "Father, the ship's sinking!" The shaft of the ship was broken.

The crippled ship, carrying hundreds of passengers, drifted helplessly away from the sea lanes. When the vessel began taking on too much water, its pumps were useless.

The crew prepared lifeboats and provisions but then began to fear that their small boats would capsize in the rough seas. So they gathered all the passengers into a main area and waited, hoping to be discovered by a passing ship.

On the second evening of their anguished wait, Moody led a prayer service that calmed many of the passengers, including himself.

Although he was sure of heaven, thoughts of his life-changing work ending and of never seeing his family again had greatly unsettled him.

Prior to the trip, a doctor had found irregularities in Moody's heart and urged him to ease his schedule or risk dying prematurely. As a result Moody had decided to slow down and scale back his plans to stage a large evangelistic event at the World's Fair.

During the crisis at sea, however, Moody believed that God was confronting him to make a decision: Would he press on with all of his might to share the life-transforming message of Christ or would he allow fear to diminish his fervor?

Ultimately, he came to the conclusion, *If God chooses to spare my life, I will work with all the power He gives me.* Realizing he might die before year's end due to his heart condition, he nevertheless trusted his life to God's care and persevered. Obviously, Moody knew and drew strength from the comforting Scripture, "All the days ordained for me were written in your book before one of them came to be."[3]

The following morning, the steamer *Lake Huron* discovered the stranded ship and towed it a thousand miles to safety. Moody pressed on with his World's Fair campaign, investing six months of unceasing labor. Consequently, "millions . . . heard the simple gospel" with "thousands genuinely converted to Christ." Moody did not die that year, nor the next, nor the next. His life was extended seven years after his perilous seafaring experience.[4]

When our lives are placed in God's hands . . . when our hope is in the reality of His promises and of His heaven . . . He will ignite our desire to shine the brightest light in this darkened world. Jesus said, "In the same way, let your light shine before others, so that they may see your good works and give glory to your Father who is in heaven."[5]

None of us knows what each day will hold or how much time we have to live. As with Moody, any catastrophe could sweep across our lives at any moment. That prompts the questions: Am I completely available to God *now*? Am I letting His light shine through me *now*? Am I willing to persevere *now*?

Be assured, many will want the light of hope in their lives when they see the light of Christ shining through your life.

## ACT II OF THE SPAFFORDS' STORY

After Anna and Horatio returned to Chicago, just walking into their silent, empty home was heartrending—seeing the girls' little shoes . . . looking at their familiar dresses. Although still awash in pain, Anna found some comfort by working with a program for needy women. Gradually, the darkness began to lift.

Horatio and Anna did have more children. Five years later Anna gave birth to a son, and two years afterward they were blessed with another daughter. But sadly, before their son's fourth birthday he contracted scarlet fever and died. For Horatio and Anna, the loss felt almost unbearable. Years later, their daughter, Bertha, reported that she never once heard her mother speak of her brother's death.

The pain of this loss was compounded by a crisis of faith. Were the children's deaths a punishment from God? Did He no longer love them? Horatio felt himself in danger of losing his faith. A year after their son's death, Anna gave birth to their last child, whom they named Grace—a gift from God following their tumultuous times of pain.

Around this time Horatio and Anna felt the need to sharpen their focus on things eternal, to refresh their walk with God, and to enrich their spiritual perspective concerning life's circumstances. And what better place for that to occur than Jerusalem. Horatio explained, "Jerusalem is where my Lord lived, suffered, and conquered. I wish to learn how to live, suffer, and especially to conquer."

Jesus met this couple at their deepest point of need. To all who are troubled He says, "Peace I leave with you; my peace I give to you. Not as the world gives do I give to you. Let not your hearts be troubled, neither let them be afraid."[6]

With several friends who also sought solace and inspiration, the Spaffords left Chicago in 1881 and moved to the Holy City. In Jerusalem the group found an environment that fascinated and uplifted them. The Spaffords and their friends rented a large house together, and due to their kindness, curiosity, and respect they quickly made friends among their neighbors.

Their home became a meeting place for local people and out-of-town visitors from all backgrounds. Both the distinguished and the destitute found a welcome hand and heart. Sometimes the destitute also found a temporary home.

The Spafford home became a lighthouse, beaming out the love of Christ. Soon His light began to shine in those around them. Like ships lost at sea and in need of safe haven, people were drawn to the Spafford home to hear the comforting words of Christ and to experience the compassionate works of Christ.

Increasingly it became clear to Horatio and Anna that they would not be returning to Chicago. Their informal ministry grew in the years ahead, and services were offered to the community. In time a wide range of outreaches and programs were added.

As Horatio, Anna, and their friends served particularly in the areas of teaching and nursing, over time they became known as the "American Colony."

The Spaffords lived out the rest of their lives in Jerusalem, continuing to serve the Lord and others. Horatio died in 1888, and Anna in 1923.

Amazingly, the comprehensive outreach initiative started by this couple still exists today but in a different form and scope. The Spafford Children's Center serves many thousands of families in Arab East Jerusalem and the West Bank, providing medical care for children from disadvantaged families. The center has also added educational, cultural, and social programs for children and their mothers.

Arriving in Jerusalem in 1881, after enduring horrific trials that battered them like hurricane-force winds, Horatio and Anna Spafford could never have envisioned the children's center that now operates in their former home.

Yet their resolute hope in the promises of God, even when tremendous storms had swept over their lives, opened the way for the center's existence and birthed a spiritual legacy that has been passed down through generations.

Countless thousands have been helped and countless more have experienced changed lives and the peace of Christ because Horatio and Anna refused to abandon their hope.[7]

## PERFECT PEACE

Horatio Spafford and D. L. Moody refused to give up hope *in* Christ, and that led to millions of people being impacted *for* Christ.

How did these men of faith keep their hope in Jesus when their lives were battered by the stormiest seas? How did they continue to stay afloat amidst the torrents of trouble?

The answer is tucked away within the pages of the book of Isaiah and particularly within one passage that today can serve as our storm shelter. When the alarm sounds—"Warning! A hurricane is about to hit your life"—take refuge in these words about the Lord:

> You keep him in perfect peace whose mind is stayed on you, because he trusts in you. Trust in the LORD forever, for the LORD GOD is an everlasting rock. (Isa. 26:3–4 ESV)

I believe the Spaffords and Moody certainly experienced doubts in their most dire circumstances, *but they didn't stay stuck there*, like a ship run aground. Their initial emotions must have churned as catastrophic events crashed down upon them, *but then they turned their minds elsewhere*. And when they looked up, focusing on the One who is sovereign over every storm, they not only found peace—they found *"perfect peace."*

*Have hope to have perfect peace.* What is perfect peace? A resolute hope rooted in the total trustworthiness of our living Savior. Those who experience perfect peace know unequivocally that there are no happenstance happenings in life apart from God's presence. God is unfolding His precise plan. Even in the pain there is purpose.

*"Trust in the LORD forever."* Note that word "forever." No matter how high the tides rise or how strong the waves break, never give up on God . . . trust in Him forever. If Horatio and Anna Spafford had given up, there would never have been a Spafford Children's Center.

*Don't focus on your circumstances.* Why focus on God, not on our circumstances? Because circumstances ebb and flow—they are always changing, unpredictable, and undependable. But in the middle of those circumstances is a Rock—our immovable, unshakable, and invincible God.

Are you in need of *perfect peace*? Is your mind swirling like an unsettled sea? Or is it steadied . . . anchored in the love and sovereignty of Christ? When you need perfect peace, turn to Isaiah 26:3–4 and consider it your storm shelter, your safe haven of hope in the most severe storms.

## *Anchoring Your Hope:*
## *Where Is Your Hope?*

Hope is something we all want . . . and something we all need. But what exactly is it? It's not peace, but it certainly produces peace.

For sure, it is something priceless. You can't buy it, earn it, or win it. You can't cause it or create it. Everyone in the world wants it, but too few have it.

The bottom line is this: Everyone wants *an anchored life,* and when you have hope, you have an anchored life. But how do you get it?

Do you realize that when you have "Christ in you, the hope of glory,"[8] that is the start of having an anchored life? Very simply, when you give Christ control of your life, He becomes your Anchor. Then, with Christ in control as your Anchor, you will have an anchored life!

How extraordinary! Always hang on to this hope: When you have Christ in you, you receive both the Anchor and the anchored life. That makes you doubly blessed . . . and doubly secure.

Now that has to give you *hope for your heart!*

# EPILOGUE: HOW TO KNOW YOUR ANCHOR WILL HOLD

What is unique about biblical hope? We've learned that this kind of hope is an undergirding force grounded in the very promises of God—guaranteed by the assurances of God.

Hundreds of classic hymns contain lines, verses, and choruses describing Jesus as our Anchor, our hope, our stay, including the hymn "In Times Like These."[a] There isn't a song I've enjoyed singing more before audiences than "In Times Like These" because it establishes what our ultimate priorities need to be in life. This song says it all (and it's simply beautiful!).

Read the lines slowly and take to heart these hope-filled truths.

> In times like these you need a Savior,
> In times like these you need an anchor;
> Be very sure, be very sure
> Your anchor holds and grips the Solid Rock!
>
> In times like these, you need the Bible,
> In times like these, O be not idle.
> Be very sure, be very sure
> Your anchor holds and grips the Solid Rock!
>
> This rock is Jesus, yes, He's the One;
> This Rock is Jesus, the only One.
> Be very sure, be very sure
> Your anchor holds and grips the Solid Rock![1]

In times like these we do have an Anchor securing us through the storms. His holding power is certain.

Rest in Him today, assured that your hope—placed in God—will never disappoint . . . will always hold . . . will anchor your life for all eternity.

---

[a] To hear "In Times Like These," "It Is Well with My Soul," and other favorite hymns recorded by June Hunt on the music CD *Hymns of Hope*, visit www.hopefortheheart.org/hymns.

# NOTES

## Part One

### Chapter One: The Ultimate Life Preserver

1. Phil. 4:13 NKJV.

2. John 8:32.

3. W. E. Vine, Merrill F. Unger, and William White, *Vine's Complete Expository Dictionary of Old and New Testament Words* (Nashville: Thomas Nelson, 1996), 2:311–312.

4. *Hurricanes . . . Unleashing Nature's Fury*, A Preparedness Guide, U.S. Department of Commerce, NOAA National Weather Service, 6.

5. Ps. 46:1–3.

### Chapter Two: When Trouble Hits Wave upon Wave

1. Matt. 26:39 ESV.

2. Exod. 20:13 KJV.

3. This event was featured on NBC's *Today* show, September 26, 2002.

4. Ps. 107:28–31.

### Chapter Three: Your Unfailing Anchor

1. Vine, Unger, and White, *Vine's Complete Expository Dictionary of Old and New Testament Words* (Nashville: Thomas Nelson, 1996), s.v. "Anchor."

2. National Safe Boating Council, "Teach and Learn: Types of Anchors," *Boatingsidekicks.com*, 2001; http://www.boatingsidekicks.com/TEACH/anchortypes.pdf.

3. Luke 5:4–5.

4. Don Casey, "Anchoring," Boat Owners Association of the United States, 2006; http://www.boatus.com/boattech/anchorin.htm.

5. Ibid.

6. Matt. 8:8 ESV.

7. See http://thinkexist.com/quotation/a_mother_is_the_truest_friend_we_have-when_trials/149949.html.

8. Casey, "Anchoring."

9. Charles Stanford, *Central Truths*, Legacy Reprint Series, originally published 1859 (Biblio Bazaar, 2009), 113.

10. Ibid.

11. For information on USS *Constitution*, see *Selected Naval Documents: USS Constitution*, "Escape from an Enemy Squadron, 1812" (Washington, DC: Department of the Navy, 1995); www.history.navy.mil/docs/war1812/const4.htm.

12. Ibid.

13. Ibid.

### Chapter Four: The Flash Floods of Affliction

1. All from ESV.

2. Acts 27:29 ESV.

3. Bernie Siegel, quoted in Richard S. Wiener, ed., *Pain Management: A Practical Guide for Clinicians* (Boca Raton, FL: CRC Press, 2001), 63.

4. Dr. Joyce O'Shaughnessy's comments were taken from an interview on the HOPE FOR THE HEART broadcast and is also on the CD album titled *Conquering the Challenge of Cancer*, available from HOPE FOR THE HEART (hopefortheheart.org).

5. Harold Koenig, *The Healing Power of Faith: How Belief and Prayer Can Help You Triumph Over Disease* (New York: Simon and Schuster, 1999), 24.

6. Ibid., 27.

7. Timothy Keller, "Preaching Amid Pluralism," *Leadership*, Winter 2002, 34–35.

8. Heb. 2:1.

### Chapter Five: The Tidal Waves of Trouble

1. H. J. Cummins, "TV or not TV," *Star Tribune* (Minneapolis), April 24, 1996.

2. Sharon Jayson, "Generation Y's Goal? Wealth and Fame," *USA Today*, January 9, 2007.

3. Ibid.

4. For information on Sam Johnson, see "Biography of U.S. Congressman Sam Johnson," http://www.samjohnson.house.gov/Biography/.

5. Todd J. Gillman, "Congressman Relives POW Experience in Vietnam," *Dallas Morning News*, January 27, 2006; http://www.samjohnson.house.gov/news/DocumentPrint.aspx?DocumentID=38841.

6. See http://www.usatoday.com/news/nation/2010–05–31-gulf-oil-spill_N.htm.

7. Robert Kiener, "Marvel of the North Atlantic," *Reader's Digest*, December 1998.

## Part Two

### *Chapter Six: Trust in the Captain's Course*

1. "How Can You Learn to Trust Again?" *Psychology Today*, March–April 2002.

2. See http://www.merriam-webster.com/netdict/captain.

3. See http://wapedia.mobi/en/Captain_%28nautical%29#2.

4. From "Invictus" by William Ernest Henley.

5. Rom. 4:18–21.

6. Inscription on walls where Jews hid from the Nazis, in Adam Fisher, *An Everlasting Name: A Service for Remembering the Shoah* (Springfield, NJ: Berhman House, 1991), 53.

### *Chapter Seven: An Anchor like No Other*

1. For information and statistics on the *Titanic*, see *Encyclopedia Titanica*, 2010, http://www.encyclopedia-titanica.org/.

2. David G. Brown, *The Last Log of the Titanic* (Encyclopedia Titanica Research, January 31, 2001); http://www.encyclopedia-titanica.org/last-log-of-the-titanic~chapter-0~part-4.html.

3. Ibid.

4. Heb. 4:13.

5. For the story of John Harper, see Elesha Coffman, "Sacrifice at Sea," http://www.christianitytoday.com/ch/news/2000/aug11.html, adapted from *The Titanic's Last Hero* (Chicago: Moody Press, 1997).

6. Ibid.

7. Luke 24:19–21.

8. Luke 24:24 esv.

9. Corrie ten Boom, as quoted in Karol Ladd, *Power of a Positive Woman* (New York: Simon and Schuster, 2002), 50.

10. Luke 24:25–27.

11. For the statistical probabilities in this section, see Peter W. Stoner and Robert C. Newman, *Science Speaks* (Chicago: Moody Press, 1963), 100–110.

12. John 3:16–17.

13. John 10:10.

14. James 4:17.

15. Isa. 59:2; Rom. 6:23.

16. Rom. 5:8.

17. John 14:6.

18. Matt. 16:24–26.

19. Eph. 2:8–9.

20. Heb. 13:8.

21. Rev. 22:16 esv.

## Chapter Eight: The Right Map Will Light Your Way

1. John 8:12.

2. Ps. 119:105 esv.

3. See June Hunt, *The Bible: Is It Reliable? Biblical Counseling Keys* (Dallas: Hope For The Heart, 2008).

4. See Henry M. Morris, *Science and the Bible*, revised and updated (Chicago: Moody, 1986), 13–14.

5. Benjamin Davidson, *The Analytical Hebrew and Chaldee Lexicon* (London: Samuel Bagster & Sons), 249. See also Ehud Ben-Yehuda and David Weinstein, *English-Hebrew, Hebrew-English Dictionary* (New York: Washington Square Press, 1961), 252.

6. Lynn Waller, *How Do We Know the Bible Is True? Reasons a Kid Can Believe It* (Grand Rapids: Zondervan, 1991), 4–5; Henry M. Morris, *The Biblical Basis for Modern Science* (Grand Rapids: Baker, 1984), 289; Answers in Genesis, "Matthew Maury's Search for the Secret of the Seas," first published in *Creation Magazine*, June 1989, www.answersingenesis.org/creation/v11/i3/maury.asp.

7. Morris, *Science and the Bible*, 11–12.

8. Ibid., 12.

9. Waller, *How Do We Know the Bible Is True?*, 8–9 and Morris, *The Biblical Basis for Modern Science*, 289.

10. H. L. Willmington, *Willmington's Guide to the Bible* (Wheaton, IL: Tyndale, 1984), 816.

11. Ibid., 817–818.

12. Ibid., 816.

13. Martin Rosenthal, "Queries and Minor Notes—Circumcision of the Newborn," *The Journal of the American Medical Association*, Vol. 133, No. 6 (February 8, 1947), 436.

14. S. I. McMillen and David Stern, *None of These Diseases* (Grand Rapids: Revell, 2003), 11.

15. Lynn Waller, *How Do We Know the Bible Is True?*, 10–11 and Morris, *The Biblical Basis for Modern Science*, 289; "Matthew Maury's Search for the Secret of the Seas."

16. Henry M. Morris, *Science and the Bible*, 14–15.

17. See Morris, *Biblical Basis for Modern Science*, 372–379.

18. McMillen and Stern, *None of These Diseases*, 15, quoted in *Willmington's Guide to the Bible*, 816.

19. Brother Andrew, *For the Love of My Brothers* (Minneapolis: Bethany House, 1998), 198.

20. Brother Andrew with John and Elizabeth Sherrill, *God's Smuggler* (Grand Rapids: Chosen Books, 2006), 30.

21. Ibid., 33.

22. Brother Andrew, *Love of My Brothers*, 15.

23. Daniel J. Boorstin, *The Discoverers* (New York: Random House, 1983), 146–147.

### Chapter Nine: Knowing How to Navigate

1. William Shakespeare, *Love's Labours Lost*, Act IV, Scene 3.

2. Source unknown.

3. 1 Thess. 5:16–18.

4. Randolph C. Byrd, M.D., "Positive Therapeutic Effects of Intercessory Prayer in a Coronary Care Unit Population," *Southern Medical Journal*, Vol. 81, No. 7 (July 1988), 826–829.

5. Dr. Byrd's clinical trial on the effects of prayer was groundbreaking and one of the first of its kind. Other subsequent studies have confirmed the link between prayer and physical and emotional healing. For more information, see *The Healing Power of Prayer* by Harold Koenig, M.D., *The Faith Factor* by Dale Matthews, M.D., and *Prayer Is Good Medicine* by Larry Dossey, M.D.

6. 2 Cor. 12:7–9.

7. Phil. 4:6.

8. Brother Lawrence, *The Practice of the Presence of God* (Boston: Shambhala Publications, 2005), 19.

9. Ibid., 23.

10. Mark Twain, *The Adventures of Huckleberry Finn* (New York: Grosset & Dunlop, 1963), 134.

11. See Joni Eareckson Tada interview with Hank Hanegraff, *Bible Answer Man* radio program, December 8, 1999; www.forgottenword.org/joni.html.

12. Ibid.

13. Ibid.

14. Ibid.

15. Joni Eareckson Tada and Steven Estes, *When God Weeps: Why Our Sufferings Matter to the Almighty* (Grand Rapids: Zondervan, 1997), 132.

## Part Three

### Chapter Ten: A Wreck Reclaimed

1. Adapted from "The Golden Age of Hymns: A Gallery of the Hymn Writers Hall of Fame," *Christian History & Biography*, No. 31, July 1, 1991, www.ctlibrary.com/ch/1991/issue31/3120.html.

2. Ibid.

3. Titus 3:7.

4. Adapted from "The Golden Age of Hymns: A Gallery of the Hymn Writers' Hall of Fame."

5. Frances Roberts, *Come Away My Beloved* (Uhrichsville, OH: Promise Press, 2002).

6. "Man Finds $40,000 Worth of Old Coins," *Billings Gazette*, October 25, 2004; http://billingsgazette.com/news/national/article_bceadf99-69f1-5ca0-a645-7234db989c49.html.

7. 2 Cor. 4:7.

### Chapter Eleven: Charting Your Course

1. *The Best of F. B. Meyer*, ed. Stephen Sorenson (Colorado Springs: Cook Communications, 2000), 168.

2. Pastor Kirbyjon Caldwell, speaking at a Willowcreek Leadership Conference; http://www.preachingtoday.com/illustrations/search.html?query=Kirbyjon+Caldwell&type=word&filter=&tone=.

3. Robert Waite, *The Psychopathic God: Adolf Hitler* (Cambridge, MA: Da Capo Press, 1993), 20.

4. Mfonobong Nsehe, *The Adolf Hitler Book: Essays, Speeches, and Quotations from Adolf Hitler* (Create Space, 2008), 25.

5. Trevor Ravenscroft, *The Spear of Destiny* (York Beach, ME: Red Wheel/Weiser, 1982), 91.

6. Hermann Rauschning, *The Voice of Destruction* (Gretna, LA: Pelican, 2003), 240.

7. Hermann Rauschning, *Men of Chaos* (New York: G. P. Putnam's Sons, 1942), 97.

8. Robert G. L. Waite, *The Psychopathic God: Adolf Hitler* (New York: Basic Books, 1977), 27.

9. George Victor, *Hitler: The Pathology of Evil* (Dulles, VA: Brassey's, 2000), 184.

### Chapter Twelve: Untangling Your Knots

1. For information on the *Arctic Rose*, see Mike Barber, "Coast Guard Makes Final Best Guess on How *Arctic Rose* Went Down," *Seattle Post-Intelligencer*, January 9, 2004, www.seattlepi.com/local/155952_rose09.html.

### Chapter Thirteen: Your Next Port: Paradise

1. Henri Nouwen, *Our Greatest Gift* (San Francisco: HarperSan-Francisco, 1994), 19–20.

2. 2 Cor. 5:1.

3. 2 Cor. 5:8 ESV.

4. Variously attributed to Henry Scott Holland and Henry Van Dyke; source uncertain.

5. Matt. 25:21.

6. John 14:2–3.

7. Rev. 21:4 ESV.

8. Ps. 16:11 ESV.

9. Job 3:17 ESV.

10. Rev. 21:27.

11. Rev. 5:11–12.

12. 2 Cor. 4:18.

13. 2 Cor. 4:16–17.

14. Ps. 30:5.

15. Lyrics by Don Wyrtzen, chorus by L.E. Singer; copyright © 1971 by Singspiration, Inc., The Zondervan Corporation.

16. 1 Cor. 2:9.

17. Phil. 3:20.

18. C. S. Lewis, *The Last Battle* (New York: HarperCollins, 1956, 1984), 227–228.

19. William Shakespeare, *Hamlet*, 3. 1.

20. Rom. 5:5.

### Chapter Fourteen: When Sea Billows Roll

1. Horatio G. Spafford, "It Is Well," public domain.

2. Phil. 4:7 esv.

3. Ps. 139:16.

4. Vinita Hampton, "The Nearly Fatal Voyage," *Christian History*, January 1, 1990, www.christianitytoday.com/ch/1990/issue25/2511.html.

5. Matt. 5:16 esv.

6. John 14:27 esv.

7. Much of this background material comes from the article by Kevin Perrotta, "It Is Well with My Soul: The Priceless Legacy of Anna and Horatio Spafford," *Word Among Us*, January 2005. Also see The Christian History Institute, Tom Corts, "Glimpses #210: Horatio Spafford: It Is Well with My Soul," Christianity Today International, July 2007, www.christianhistorytimeline.com/GLIMPSEF/Glimpses2/glimpses210.html; Forrest McCann, *Hymns and History* (Abilene, TX: Abilene Christian University Press, 1997).

8. Col. 1:27.

### Epilogue: How to Know Your Anchor Will Hold

1. Ruth Caye Jones, "In Times Like These," quoted in Kenneth W. Osbeck, *101 More Hymn Stories: The Inspiring True Stories Behind 101 Favorite Hymns* (Grand Rapids: Kregel, 1985), #46.

# ABOUT THE AUTHOR

June Hunt is an author, singer, speaker, and founder of HOPE FOR THE HEART, a worldwide biblical counseling ministry featuring the award-winning radio broadcast by the same name heard daily across America. In addition, HOPE IN THE NIGHT is June's live two-hour call-in counseling program that helps people untie their tangled problems with biblical hope and practical help. HOPE FOR THE HEART'S radio broadcasts air on approximately four hundred radio outlets worldwide.

Early family pain was the catalyst that shaped June's compassionate heart. Later, as a youth director for more than six hundred teenagers, she became aware of the need for sound biblical counseling. Her work with young people and their parents led June to a life commitment of providing *God's Truth for Today's Problems*.

After years of teaching and research, June began developing scripturally based counseling tools called *Biblical Counseling Keys* that address definitions, characteristics, causes, and steps to solutions for a hundred topics (such as marriage and parenting, anger and abuse, guilt and grief). Recently these individual topics were compiled to create the landmark *Biblical Counseling Library*.

The Counseling Keys have become the foundation for the HOPE FOR THE HEART'S *Biblical Counseling Institute*, initiated by The Criswell College. Each monthly conference in the Dallas-based Institute provides training to help spiritual leaders, counselors, and other caring Christians meet the very real needs of others.

June has served as a guest professor at colleges and seminaries, both nationally and internationally, teaching on topics such as crisis counseling, child abuse, wife abuse, homosexuality, forgiveness, singleness, and self-worth. Her works are currently available in more than sixty countries and more than twenty languages, including Russian, Romanian, Ukrainian, Spanish, Portuguese, German, Mandarin, Korean, Japanese, and Arabic.

She is the author of *How to Forgive . . . When You Don't Feel Like it, Seeing Yourself Through God's Eyes, Bonding with Your Teen through Boundaries, How to Rise Above Abuse, Counseling Through Your Bible Handbook, How to Handle Your Emotions, Keeping Your Cool . . . When Your Anger Is Hot!, Caring for a Loved One with Cancer,* and more than forty topical HopeBooks. June is also a contributor to the *Soul Care Bible* and the *Women's Devotional Bible.*

An accomplished musician, June has been a guest on numerous national television and radio programs, including the NBC *Today* show. She has toured overseas with the USO and has been a guest soloist at Billy Graham crusades. Five recordings—*Songs of Surrender, Hymns of Hope, The Whisper of My Heart, The Shelter Under His Wings,* and *The* HOPE *of Christmas*—all reflect her heart of hope.

Learn more about June and HOPE FOR THE HEART at:

**www.HopeForTheHeart.org**
**2001 W. Plano Parkway, Suite 1000**
**Plano, TX 75075**
**800-488-HOPE (4673)**

*Hope for Your Heart: Finding Strength in Life's Storms* by June Hunt.